Ts'ai Yüan-p'ei

The Pennsylvania
State University
Studies No. 41

Ts'ai Yüan-p'ei
Educator of Modern China

by William J. Duiker

The Pennsylvania State University Press
University Park and London

Library of Congress Cataloging in Publication Data

Duiker, William J   1932-
  Ts'ai Yüan-p'ei, educator of modern China.

  (The Pennsylvania State University studies; no. 41)
  Includes bibliographical references.
  1. Ts'ai, Yüan p'ei, 1867–1940.   2.   Educators—China
—Biography. 3.   Education—China—History.   4.   Ts'ai,
Yüan-p'ei, 1867–1940—Knowledge—Education.   I.   Series:
Pennsylvania. State University. The Pennsylvania State
University studies; no. 41
LA2383. C52T753   370'.92'4 [B]   77-1748
ISBN 0-271-00504-1

Designed by Glenn Ruby

Printed in the United States of America

To My Mother and the Memory of My Father

Contents

Preface

Since I first envisioned this study, I have become indebted to several people who have helped me in various ways. Professor James T. C. Liu provided some initial suggestions while my research was in its formative stages. Others who have given me assistance at various steps are Michael Gasster, Don Price, Director Wan-li Chu of the National Central Library in Taipei, who helped me to locate recent materials on Taiwan, and Doctor Sun Te-chung, editor of many compilations of the writings of Ts'ai Yüan-p'ei. Also helpful were T'ao Ying-hui and Li Nien-hsuan of the Institute of Modern History at the Academia Sinica. Professor John K. Fairbank kindly made a number of suggestions which improved the quality of the manuscript. I would like to thank Mrs. Ilene Glenn for her typing and editorial assistance. I am especially grateful to Doctor Wei-kuo Lee of Georgetown University for his assistance while this work was in its dissertation stage, and to Doctor Thomas Helde and Father Joseph Sebes, S. J., who patiently read the manuscript and made a number of useful suggestions. I have received financial assistance from the Institute for the Arts and Humanistic Studies and from the College Fund for Research of the College of Liberal Arts at The Pennsylvania State University for help in bringing this work to completion, and I am grateful for their aid.

Finally, I would like to give special thanks to my wife, Yvonne, for her endless patience and encouragement during a period in which Ts'ai Yüan-p'ei seemed, all too often, to become a member of the family.

1

Introduction

China's struggle to meet the challenge of the Western world has been a subject of enduring scholarly interest in recent years. This struggle has been cultural and intellectual in scope as well as political and social, involving not only the decline and ultimate disintegration of traditional political and social institutions but also the destruction of an existing intellectual world. A nation has been forced to abandon its traditional sense of cultural identity and to construct another in its place.

The challenge of this cultural transformation was especially difficult for the transitional generation of Chinese that was raised and educated in a world of Confucian traditions, but saw in early maturity the failure of existing institutions to forestall defeat and humiliation. Furthermore, they often observed evidence of the apparent superiority of Western culture to their own. Not by coincidence, this generation has been the subject of several biographical studies in which the complexity of the cultural conflict between China and the West is explored. As testimony to this enduring fascination, biographical works about the following transitional figures have been recently published: Liang Ch'i-ch'ao, Sun Yat-sen, K'ang Yu-wei, Yen Fu, Sung Chiao-jen, and Huang Hsing.

This study of the Chinese moral philosopher and educator Ts'ai Yüan-p'ei is a further contribution to the scholarship on this period. Born in Chekiang Province in 1868, Ts'ai grew up in a predominantly traditional society. Ambitious and intelligent, he prospered under the Confucian educational system, and by his early twenties he had attained membership in the Hanlin Academy. By the end of the century, however, Ts'ai Yüan-p'ei had lost faith in the old values. In 1907, after spending several years as a revolutionary in Shanghai, he left China for Europe, determined to discover the true secret of Western success. Ultimately, he would spend over a decade in Europe absorbing the knowledge of the West. Few Chinese were in a better position to interpret Western civilization to the East.

The influence of Western thought upon Ts'ai Yüan-p'ei was crucial; once exposed to European civilization he adhered to a vision of life fashioned by the advance in science and in democratic values in the modern West. Yet, the delicate strains of Confucianism were not entirely muted. Though a determined opponent of traditional ritualism

1

and attitudes, he also represented by his conduct and beliefs the finest tradition of the Confucian gentleman. Here indeed the attempt to create a new China based on a synthesis of traditional values with Western concepts would find one of its finest advocates.

In this respect, Ts'ai can be viewed as a representative of his age, symbolizing the dilemmas of an intellectual caught between the cultural worlds of East and West. As interest in the Sino-Western cultural confrontation demonstrates, there is more to the issue than the exchange of one cultural system for another. Cultural and intellectual ideas exist at many levels—from manifestations in the domain of ritual and institutions to the deeper level of ethical and social values, and finally down to the core of a culture, the inner assumptions about the ultimate nature of man, the universe, and reality itself. In most cases, these values and attitudes are consciously held and are recognized as part of the existing political and cultural heritage. They can be retained or rejected by the individual as he chooses aspects of the traditional order which he wishes to keep or abandon. In other cases, however, these perceptions exist at the subliminal level and may influence the behavior and attitudes of an individual without his being aware of them. A radical, even in the process of selecting ideas from the outside, may be unconsciously influenced by assumptions inherited from the traditional culture. Moreover, the cultural conflict between China and the modern West is not simply a two-dimensional clash between two self-contained civilizations. As Professor Hao Chang has stated in his study of Liang Ch'i-ch'ao, the Chinese intellectual world of the late nineteenth century was by no means a cultural monolith, but a variegated complex of attitudes and concerns centered around some basic questions regarding the nature of man, society, and the universe.[1] In the broadest sense, to be a Confucian meant to share certain assumptions and attitudes, to ask philosophical questions in a certain way, and to look at life through a Confucian prism, so to speak. Generalizations along these lines are dangerous, however, for Confucian thought contained a number of inner tensions, basic disagreements over fundamental questions extending to the deepest elements of the traditional world view.[2] If Confucianism, or that current of the Master's teachings carried down by Mencius and the Neo-Confucianists of the Sung dynasty and after, stressed the necessity for a world view and a humanistic approach to society's problems, a more pragmatic approach had developed around Hsün Tzu and the quasi-legalists, and eventually was assimilated into the Chinese bloodstream through the State Confucian tradition in imperial China.

These contrasting views are too familiar to need elaboration here. Suffice it to say that the Mencian tradition based its philosophy on a belief in the goodness of man and the importance of the individual in the structure of human society. Humanists admitted that government

2

would occasionally be forced to rely on coercion to realize social goals.[3] But they placed emphasis on the voluntary nature of man's obligation to his community. For Hsün Tzu and others, however, man by nature was evil or a mere bundle of instincts. The ordering of society, therefore, cannot come solely through the Confucian virtues of self-cultivation or virtuous example by those in authority, but must be imposed from above by government policy. In this case, stress would be placed on discipline and the force of law in order to coerce individuals to follow the Way. As with the humanists, the final goal might still be the people's welfare, the realization of which would be primarily dependent upon political action rather than voluntary self-cultivation. Building a strong state would be of primary concern, not developing the concept of individual freedom. Put simply, the humanists stressed the primacy of ethics, the quasi-legalists, the primacy of politics.[4] The nature of the controversy changed over the centuries, but defenders of each point of view found the distinction meaningful down to the intellectual conflicts of the Ch'ing dynasty. If the humanist attitude dominated the world of scholarship and education, quasi-legalism was very much alive in the world of the bureaucracy.

The implications of this tension within Confucian thought are not without importance to the student of the Chinese Cultural Revolution of the twentieth century. As Chinese intellectuals reacted to Western ideas, they responded in terms of their own humanist or quasi-legalist leanings, as absorbed through traditional thought. Previous studies, for example, have demonstrated that the quasi-legalist predilections of progressives such as Liang Ch'i-ch'ao and Yen Fu led them to accept the relatively mechanistic assumptions of Western social Darwinist theory. By contrast, Ts'ai Yüan-p'ei, perhaps better than any of his contemporaries, reflected in his thought the humanist strain in traditional Confucian philosophy. Intensely moral, preoccupied with questions relating to the ethical and spiritual side of human life, Ts'ai carried this humanist orientation in his intellectual and emotional baggage as he approached Western thought and found himself responding favorably to the humanistic side of Western culture. With Ts'ai, as with Liang and Yen Fu, the Confucian outlook had increasingly given way to a Western world view, but at the inner core, Confucian tradition has been served.

As this study will attempt to make clear, there is more to cultural change than the simple abandonment of the Chinese Confucian essence [the *t'i*] and the adoption of Western scientific civilization [the *yung*]. The Chinese Cultural Revolution, therefore, involved changes in the minds of men—in their values and attitudes, and in their deepest beliefs about the meaning of life around them. This conflict of ideas is one element of the revolution which has shaken China in our century. Ts'ai Yüan-p'ei's life and thought form one aspect of that story.

3

2

From Confucian Scholar
to Radical Reformer

The Formative Years. The childhood of Ts'ai Yüan-p'ei, as seen through the biographical essays that are familiar to students of Chinese history, must have been similar to that of millions of Chinese boys since the beginning of Chinese culture. Readers of such sketches may be struck by the timeless quality of the youthful experiences described—the father determined to give his son the educational opportunities he himself had lacked, and the painful years spent in learning the Confucian classics by rote with the aid of a local scholar. Such a childhood might have as easily occurred during the Sung dynasty as during the last half of the nineteenth century.

In the past, traditional accounts of the lives of prominent Chinese usually contained an outline of the man in the boy, in order to show academic leanings in the potential scholar, a youthful bravado in the future warrior. So it was in the accounts of Ts'ai's childhood. Born in the sunset years of Confucian civilization, he was exposed to the traditional educational system. Authors of accounts of his boyhood, aware of his later achievements in scholarship, proudly point to early indications of Ts'ai's ability and interest in learning. One author provides an almost Lincolnesque picture of the young boy as he studies by the light of the ashes in the kitchen stove.[1] Others, keeping in mind his lifelong concern for ethical behavior, emphasize his piety and willingness to sacrifice for his family. One often wonders how much of this simply reveals a natural desire to show the relevance of early training to adult behavior. Ts'ai's youthful love of learning and moral fervor, however, seem to be well documented and can be accepted as an accurate portrayal of his early character.

Ts'ai Yüan-p'ei (courtesy name Chieh-min) was born on 12 January 1868 during the reign of Emperor T'ung-chih in Chekiang Province.[2] His father, Ts'ai Kuang-p'u, was the manager of a *ch'ien-chuang*, the old-style Chinese bank. According to tradition, Ts'ai's ancestors had been gatherers of firewood until one of them was wounded by a hatchet in the hands of a competitor. Ts'ai's father was one of seven brothers, most of whom had become merchants. One had earned a baccalaureate degree [*hsiu-ts'ai*], the first member of the family to attain such a civil-service standing.[3] Although he was not wealthy, Ts'ai's father engaged a local scholar to tutor the young boy in the traditional way at home. When young Ts'ai was eleven, however, his father died and left the family with only meager savings. Consequently, the domestic schooling had to be temporarily abandoned. His mother worked to support her family rather than accept financial help from friends and relatives.[4] She did agree, however, to send Ts'ai to study with his scholarly uncle, Ts'ai Ming-shan. Since the boy had been exposed to traditional Confucian texts from the age of five, he soon began to show definite talent for scholarship.[5] After studying with his uncle for two years, he began to study with Wang Tzu-chuang, a local scholar from whom he learned the eight-legged essay style and Sung Neo-Confucianism.[6]

After passing the first civil-service examination at age seventeen, Ts'ai became a *hsiu-ts'ai* and tutored children while continuing his studies. In 1889, he received a master of arts degree [*chü-jen*] and a year later passed the examination for the doctorate [*chin-shih*].[7] During this time he worked as chief historiographer, first in the Shanghai district and then in the province of Chekiang. In 1892, he became a Hanlin scholar and joined that illustrious academy in 1894 as a compiler [*pien-hsiu*]. Ts'ai had attained the highest honor accorded to the scholar in traditional China.[8]

Unfortunately, we know little about Ts'ai's youthful years, his family, his character, and his social environment. Such information might provide us with insight into his later intellectual development. In the traditional accounts, unfortunately, we are limited to glimpses of his love of scholarship and his concern for moral principles. Of his dedication to high ideals which characterized his later life and made him such a distinctive personality in republican China, we obtain only occasional indications.

Ts'ai's preoccupation with content rather than style, with fundamentals rather than details, led him to search for the basic meaning in Chinese classical literature and influenced the character of his approach to Confucian philosophy. Never at home with scholastic squabbles over detail, he concentrated on the broad meaning behind the Confucian classics and emphasized synthesis and points of similarity rather than differences. What, then, were the elements of Confucian thought that shaped Ts'ai's world view on the eve of his exposure to the West? Perhaps a summary of the core elements in traditional Confucian philosophy would be helpful here:

1. Belief in the existence of a moral core to the universe. In Confucian doctrine, this ethico-spiritual source was not conceived of as an anthropomorphic deity as in the Christian West, but as an impersonal force, a Chinese version of the Western concept of a law of nature. In its Chinese equivalent, however, this impersonal heaven had vague moral connotations and was considered purposeful and rational.

2. A worldly concern with man and society. Although Confucian doctrine affirmed man's ability to comprehend the nature of reality, of truth, and of the basic moral laws of the universe [the *Tao*], it also reflected Confucius's view that speculation on metaphysics was fruitless, and thus directed its primary attention toward problems of constructing a good society on earth. Some interest in metaphysics was present, however, and attracted concern, particularly during the Sung dynasty.

3. A preoccupation with ethics. Concerned with the establishment of rules governing relations among men in society, the Confucianist devoted his major attention to problems of ethics; Confucian doctrine, above all, came to be viewed as a philosophy of ethics. To say this is not to deny Confucian interest in other questions. But where knowledge has been of great importance in Western philosophy, ethics has traditionally had the highest priority in China.

4. A positivist belief in the efficacy of social action. Confucian philosophy saw the problem of ethics on two levels, personal ethics [self-cultivation, or *hsiu-shen*] and social ethics [service to society, or *chih-kuo p'ing t'ien-hsia*]. Following *Ta hsüeh* ("Great Learning"), Confucian doctrine asserted that morality begins with the self, and extends to the family and ultimately to all human beings in society. Ethics, therefore, was a matter of priorities and gradations. Personal knowledge of morality, however, was seen as irrevocably tied to social action, although the fundamental relationship between the two concepts was often debated among Confucian scholars. Further, Confucianists believed that social action in society could improve conditions in the world of man. The phenomenal world was no illusion, but was the practical plane on which human life must be led. The Chinese did not believe that man had total control over his own destiny because much was affected by fate [*ming*], and there was no recognizable doctrine of progress in Chinese thought. But man, by his own action, could often improve the world around him.

5. Belief in the inherent goodness of man. Faith in the potential goodness of human nature was part of the Confucianist's makeup. In some cases, this belief was tempered with skepticism, and some scholars denied the assumption altogether. Most, however, accepted the proposition as a workable assumption, and it underlay the Confucianist's optimistic viewpoint toward society. On a practical basis, this assumption was tempered by realism. Some men [the *chün tzu*] could be brought to follow the Way by education and self-cultivation. For most, however, ethical training had to be supplemented by laws.

6. Belief in the individual's importance in human society. This proposition sometimes seems difficult to hold because of the fundamental authoritarianism of the Confucian state. Political authoritarianism, however, does not conflict entirely with a broad recognition that the

welfare of the individual is the central concern of government. Since in Confucian belief, most men could not adequately govern themselves, the individual was normally a passive recipient, rather than an active participant. Nevertheless, authoritarianism was limited by the concept that the emperor was also subject to the *Tao,* and could be removed if he failed to conform to it.

Within this broad spectrum of belief, there was room for disagreement, and some Confucianists might question some of the core elements. As for Ts'ai's views, our knowledge of his early approach to Confucianism is limited, and we cannot at this time seriously evaluate his attitude toward the inner conflicts in Confucian philosophy. From what is available, however, we can piece together his general attitude. With his concern for content and broad principles, it is apparent that he avoided the sterile conflicts over interpretation that characterized the approach of many Confucian schools during the late Ch'ing period. Nor was he attracted to the scholasticism of the School of Textual Research (Han Learning). Ts'ai was more concerned with the fundamental problem of bringing these broad moral principles to bear on the self and on society.[9]

The nature of Ts'ai's early Confucianism is indicated in his admiration for a group of obscure scholars in his own district—the Shao-hsing Study Society [*Shao-hsing Chih-hsüeh Hui*]. These scholars had attempted to attain the three ethical goals of ending poverty, sickness, and evil [the "three great desires," or *san ta-yüan*] on earth. Most of Ts'ai's friends during his early manhood were interested in the School of Textual Research and mocked the "three great desires" as visionary. Ts'ai, however, felt that there was truth in the simple concept and later confessed that the influence of these principles never left him.[10]

A final work of historical scholarship which he enjoyed was the *Kung-yang Commentary,* the classic which had been held up by K'ang Yu-wei to support the contention that Confucius was a prophet as well as a philosopher, and had anticipated an era of peace and democracy. Perhaps the most striking aspect was the concept of the *Ta-t'ung* ("Great Unity"), a three-stage process by which mankind would proceed to the ultimate paradise, a concept of unilinear progress somewhat unusual in China. Ts'ai liked the idea and often alluded to the *Ta-t'ung* in later years.

In sum, Ts'ai reached manhood with a broad concern for ethics within the framework of a Confucian rational universe. The need for order, harmony, and the ultimate goodness of man was strongly ingrained in his thought. Ts'ai was committed to the dual goals of self-cultivation and service to the community, but was apparently convinced that the true road for the Confucian *chün tzu* was dedication to social reform and the realization of the *Ta-t'ung.* These concepts were to remain the cornerstones of his thought during his mature life.

The Activist Years. In 1898, while Ts'ai was a young bureaucrat in Peking, he was unhappy about China's recent humiliations at the hands of foreign powers, in particular at her defeat in 1895 by Japan. In 1898, attracted by the Japanese example, he and a number of friends set up a school in Peking to teach the Japanese language.[11] He was also sympathetic to K'ang Yu-wei and his proposals for constitutional reform. Since he was not acquainted with K'ang or his colleagues, Ts'ai may have decided not to participate actively in the movement. Perhaps he was simply being circumspect. As a source of the times remarked, "the reformers were hot to the touch, and anyone associated with them could easily be burned."[12]

When the reformers were defeated, Ts'ai resigned angrily from the Hanlin Academy and returned to Shao-hsing district, where he became supervisor [*ching-tu*] of the East-West School [*Chung-hsi Hsüeh-t'ang*].[13] The events in Peking had deeply impressed him. Prior to the movement he apparently had not formulated his ideas beyond the vague hopes for reform within the traditional system. Now that K'ang's movement to attain changes with the assistance of the court had failed, Ts'ai began to feel that change within the dynastic system was a vain hope.[14] K'ang Yu-wei's program had failed, he concluded, because the reformers had erroneously believed that a group of progressives could change a corrupt government and modernize a nation through a simple *coup d'état*. Modernization could take place only through the creation of a strong reform party based on mass support, aiming at the destruction of the old dynasty.[15] Ts'ai was aware of the moderates' argument that the Chinese people were not ready for democracy and social change. Consequently, he saw that education of the masses and the importation of Western thought were essential to the creation of a new China. Despite his exposure to Confucian tradition and his success in Peking, Ts'ai lost faith in the reformist approach. Later, his assistant at Peking University, Chiang Monlin, recalled that during a dinner at the East-West School Ts'ai had become emotional in his criticism of the dynasty and of the moderates, and had insisted that reform would be impossible without the overthrow of the dynasty. In the early 1900s, a number of publications appeared in Chinese about socialism, nihilism, and anarchism, and Ts'ai began reading Japanese translations of Western works on these subjects.[16]

The East-West School was his first experience with a modern educational institution. Established by public funds, the school included in its curriculum philosophy, literature, and history, as well as English and French. The highly progressive views of the students were shared by many members of the faculty. Ts'ai and two teaching colleagues, Ma Yung-hsi and Tu Ye-ch'uan, began to advocate their radical ideas among students, proposing school reforms and arguing politics with the more conservative elements in the school. Ma was an advocate of human rights and female emancipation, while Tu supported Western evolutionary theory.[17] Resentful conservatives informed school authorities, however, and Ts'ai was instructed to display in classrooms the imperial decree on loyal behavior. Humiliated, he resigned his position and took up a new post at the South Seas Public School [Nan-yang Kung-hsüeh-hsiao] in Shanghai as a teacher of Japanese.[18]

Ts'ai's move to the school was a fateful one which placed him in the center of the most active revolutionary movement in China. Shanghai, under Western influence, had become a commercial center and the focus of Western thought in China. Intellectuals began to settle there, attracted not only by the cosmopolitan atmosphere, but also by the legal advantages offered to foreigners. Schools which taught foreign subjects began to appear in the early 1900s and students and faculty alike voiced their dissatisfactions with events in China. Among such institutions was the South Seas School.

By 1902, Shanghai had become the focus of dissident feelings throughout central China, and radicals began to congregate in the bustling metropolis to share their discontents: Wu Chih-hui, recently returned from Japan and later to become an anarchist and Kuomintang party stalwart; Chang T'ai-yen, a Confucian scholar but anti-Manchu in his politics; and the Buddhist reformer Huang Tsung-yang. On Ts'ai's arrival, the dissidents had not yet organized, nor were they openly revolutionary. But their discontent with conditions was growing and began to be expressed: students and progressive faculty were distressed at conservative administrative policies in many of the schools in Shanghai; and progressives were resentful at the Manchu court's failure to institute internal reforms to halt the deterioration of China's international position.

During the spring of 1902, this disparate sentiment was organized with the formation of the Chinese Educational Association [Chung-kuo Chiao-yü-hui].[19] The founders, among whom Ts'ai and Wu were prominent, were mainly teachers who shared a common belief in the importance of education in the struggle for Chinese revival. At the outset they encouraged the improvement of textbooks and of educational methods in China. Wu was especially determined to create schools which would bring about changes in Chinese society. Soon, however, the new association would possess a more general aim—the organization and promotion of revolution.[20] Ts'ai, as one of its founders, became the president. The association began to attract other radicals in the area and became the focus of revolutionary sentiment in Shanghai.

Inevitably, the radical wave began to affect conditions at other schools in Shanghai. At the South Seas School, student discontent with pedagogical authoritarianism was growing, and in the fall of 1902, a student strike against the dictatorial methods of some of the instructors took place. When school authorities refused to satisfy their demands, a number of progressive teachers and students resigned. Ts'ai himself, an advocate of students' rights, sided with the students and resigned along with them. In 1901, he and Chang Chih-yü had formed the Patriotic Girls' School [*Ai-kuo Nü-hsüeh-hsiao*], and when the students from the South Seas School resigned, Ts'ai arranged for financial aid from the Educational Association to set up a school to accommodate the students. Keeping the original name of the girls' school he called it the Patriotic Academy [*Ai-kuo Hsüeh-she*]. Several members of the association became teachers at the new school, which gained renown among revolutionary groups throughout Shanghai.[21]

By now, the radicals' goals had become openly revolutionary. At the Patriotic Academy, teachers advocated revolution and prepared for insurrection by teaching revolutionary history and arranging for military training. Outside the school, radicals arranged mass meetings to encourage institutional changes, and they protested against the alleged failure of the Manchu government to undertake needed reforms in Chinese society. The radicals met at the famous *Chang-yüan,* a large park often used for political speeches.[22] Ts'ai, Wu, and others often protested at *Chang-yüan* against Russian advances in Manchuria and against rumors that local warlords in southern China were planning to pass control of the area to France.[23] By the spring of 1903, radical activities in Shanghai came to a head with the organization of groups designed specifically to organize resistance against foreign aggression.

Spring was destined to be the high-water mark for the revolutionary movement in Shanghai for two reasons: a split in the movement itself and a clampdown by the Manchu governmental authorities. By early 1903, a disagreement occurred between members of the Educational Association and students and their supporters at the Patriotic Academy. Evidently the feud originated in financial disagreements but was exacerbated by ideological differences and a bitter clash between two of the leaders, Wu Chih-hui and Chang T'ai-yen. In late spring, attempts to heal the breach failed, and the two organizations severed their connection. Ts'ai took advantage of the disagreement and left for Tsing-tao in Shantung Province to study German.[24]

The government's decision to take action against the radical movement in Shanghai was prompted, however, by the outspoken views expressed by its radical mouthpiece, the *Kiangsu Journal* [*Su-pao*]. The *Su-pao* had been established in 1896, but in 1902 it formed a liaison with the Patriotic Academy and became for the first time a revolutionary journal.[25] In 1903, Chang Shih-chao, a radical politician, became editor of the newspaper, and many of its articles grew increasingly anti-Manchu in tone. With the self-righteousness of the revolutionary fanatic, many radicals not only opposed the Manchu dynasty, but had a burning contempt for reformers such as K'ang Yu-wei who attempted to reform from the inside. K'ang had written articles elsewhere deriding the revolutionaries for their anti-Manchu sentiment and defended his own thesis that the government could be persuaded to adopt constitutionalism. Chang T'ai-yen replied with a blistering article criticizing K'ang's approach, and Chang Shih-chao placed it in the journal. Another member of the academy, Tsou Jung, had written a revolutionary pamphlet entitled *The Revolutionary Army* [*Ko-ming-chün*], and a prefatory piece by Chang T'ai-yen was also printed in the *Su-pao*, in which Chang included an insult to the emperor and asked: "How can we have a revolution without getting rid of the hereditary monarchy?"

The Manchu authorities had attempted to repress the radical movement. At one time, a spy was instructed to lure Ts'ai and Wu to make inflammatory statements within Chinese territory. They were unsuccessful, however, because some of the local officials sympathized with the revolutionaries, and also because the radicals operated in the Shanghai foreign concession area in which the Chinese government had no right to arrest the instigators openly.[26] The viceroy of Nanking was ordered to seize the revolutionaries and have them executed. Ultimately, the Chinese government asked the Shanghai foreign settlement consular authorities to arrest and extradite the leaders to China.[27] The consular authorities gave their approval. The Shanghai Municipal Council [*kung-pu-chü*] did not, however, claiming that it would arrest anyone planning a revolt but not those simply making inflammatory speeches. Eventually, the Municipal Council agreed that some of the writings in the *Su-pao*—particularly Chang T'ai-yen's preface—were inciting in tone and agreed on a compromise. Chang and Tsou Jung were arrested by foreign settlement police, placed on trial, and sentenced to prison. Consequently, the *Su-pao* and the Patriotic Academy were closed, and the revolutionaries temporarily scattered.

The *Su-pao* incident was an interlude in Ts'ai's activities in Shanghai. He did not remain for long in Tsing-tao, moving back to Peking in mid-1903, where he got in touch with an old friend, Liu Hun. In turn, Liu reprimanded him for his rebellious activities in Shanghai. After hiding him briefly, Liu eventually found Ts'ai a job in the German language department at the Translation Bureau [*I-hsüeh-kuan*]. A number of Ts'ai's old friends knew of his presence in Peking and offered to help him. Some of his official contacts, however, were nervous, since hiding a radical was a serious offense, and Ts'ai was eventually pressured into resigning and leaving the capital. Ts'ai returned to Shanghai and, after translating Japanese materials for a brief period, restored his contacts with the revolutionaries.[28]

By 1904, Ts'ai was again deep in political activities. The Girls' School had survived the debacle of the *Su-pao* period, and he returned to the school as director. Ts'ai became acquainted with an ex-resident of Kansu Province and member of the Educational Association, Ch'en Ching-ch'uan, who wanted to invest funds for a new revolutionary journal. Concern in China continued over Russia's failure to remove its occupation troops from Manchuria, where they were stationed following the Boxer Rebellion. Ts'ai, with Ch'en, Wang Hsiu-hsü, and Wang Yün-tsung, decided to establish a newspaper which would not only warn the nation against the danger of a Russian invasion, but would also spread revolutionary sentiment. The *E-shih ching-wen* [Important News about Russia] began publication in December, devoting the major part of its space and effort to events in the North, but also attempting to inculcate revolutionary spirit in its readers by teaching the history of Russian nihilism.[29] In addition to its diatribes against Russian activities, it published inflammatory pictures of alleged Russian atrocities committed on Chinese citizens. When the Russo-Japanese War began, the name of the paper was changed to *Ching-chung jih-pao* [Alarm Bell Daily News]. It related the events of the war and maintained a strongly nationalist pose. Ts'ai, sometime editor of the paper, published anti-Russian articles under pseudonyms.[30] The newspaper had a limited circulation, however, since it did not print ordinary news. Eventually, for lack of funds, Ts'ai resigned from the paper in order to concentrate his activities at the Girls' School. Liu Shih-p'ei, soon to become a prominent anarchist in Japan, took over the paper, which was ultimately closed down by Shanghai municipal authorities in January 1905.

During this period, Ts'ai was engaged in more direct revolutionary activities. As the dispersal of the *Chang-yüan* group began, a number of rebels, some returning from Japan where anti-Manchu and anti-Russian activity was flourishing among Chinese students, attempted to create new organizations to further their plans. One of the rebels, Kung Pao-ch'uan (Wei-sheng), was a friend of Ts'ai's who wanted to establish a new organization in the Shanghai area. In the fall of 1904, he told Ts'ai of his plans to set up a network at the behest of Chinese rebels in Japan and asked him to participate. Ts'ai agreed to join the new organization which was named the Restoration Society [*Kuang-fu-hui*].

In a short time, he became head of the new society, which obtained the talents of local activists as well as returnees from Japan such as T'ao Ch'eng-chang and Hsü Hsi-lin.[31] The organization also contained a smaller body devoted to perfecting the art of assassination, a product of China's new knowledge of Russian nihilist tactics. This team, originally led by Ho Hai-ch'iao, Yang Shou-jen (Tu-sheng), and Su Feng-chu, all recently arrived from Tokyo, rented a room in Shanghai where they created explosives for use in assassination attempts against Manchu officials. Ts'ai met the group and took their work seriously, for he made an effort to train assassination teams made up of the girl students at the school.[32]

Neither the Restoration Society nor the assassination team was successful. Several sources comment that Ts'ai as chairman of the society was a poor administrator and strategist; consequently, the affairs of the group did not prosper.[33] Eventually, Hsü Hsi-lin moved to Shao-hsing to teach at the Great Harmony School [*Ta-t'ung Hsüeh-t'ang*]; shortly after, Kung and T'ao followed him, taking the society's headquarters with them. Apparently, the assassination team collapsed for lack of funds.

Although the Shanghai revolutionaries were unsuccessful, the year 1905 was a turning point in the fortunes of the Chinese revolutionary movement. In that year, Sun Yat-sen's alliance of revolutionary groups, the *T'ung-meng-hui* ("The Revolutionary Alliance"), was formed in Tokyo. The Restoration Society contacted Sun's group and many of its members joined the alliance, establishing a new branch in Shanghai which was headed by Ts'ai.[34] His period of active participation in the new organization was brief, however. He became discouraged and resigned his leadership as well as his position at the Patriotic Girls' School. Shortly after, Ts'ai accepted a position with the Translation Bureau in Peking, this time as teacher of Western history and Chinese literature. But he would soon leave China for an extended period of study.

Lack of material makes it difficult to assess this period of his life, and we have relatively little information about his personal views at that time. Before the 1911 revolution Ts'ai did little writing, and we have only sketchy indications of his reaction to events in China. Like most of his colleagues, he was motivated by a strong sense of nationalism. This sentiment, however, was not tinged with racist overtones. In an early article in the *Su-pao,* he had criticized the movement's desire to oppose the Manchus for racist reasons.[35] Nor was he a simple patriot, for the utopianism of his early belief in the *Ta-t'ung* was gradually enriched by Western radical thought. By 1903, he had been exposed to socialist and nihilist thought from Russia and was beginning to express his ideals in terms of "from each according to his ability, to each according to his need." To this vague communism he added another ideal, the abolition of the joint family system. His beliefs were clearly stated in the short story "Dream of a New Year" in which he hypothesized a utopian world almost Orwellian in its proportions.

Significantly, however, Ts'ai never joined a socialist movement. He had little respect for the socialists in China who, in his view, were shiftless, greedy, and unprincipled. Communism, he concluded, would be achieved when the desire for private profit was eliminated,

13

and the family system could be abolished when adultery was no longer practiced.[36] In other words, moral transformation had to precede social reform. Although he still believed in the Communist ideal, Ts'ai turned his attention to education, which in his mind would spur the progress of mankind.

His nationalism, too, was already diluted by a broader vision which distinguished him from his colleagues. Ts'ai often asked his students at the South Seas School whether world morality was likely to increase along with material progress. Ts'ai's own response to this question is not clear, but his advice to the students was in a familiar vein: to build a better world you should start with yourself and then extend your concern to the nation, and, finally, to the whole world.[37] This concern for personal morality and inner longing for an ethical universe may be viewed as the remnants of Ts'ai's disintegrating Confucian world view, a desire to temper the nationalism of the Chinese revolutionary movement with the moral veneer of Confucian universalism. These questions reflected the concerns and solutions which would naturally occur to a Confucian intellectual confronted with the problems of late nineteenth-century China. Evidently, Ts'ai was trying to reconcile social change along Western lines with the passionate concern for ethics that characterized his youthful thought.

By the age of thirty-eight, Ts'ai had amassed the ingredients of a distinctive philosophy of life, but they were still in a rudimentary form. But he could not tolerate such theoretical confusion. His penchant to strike at the root of the problem, to relate philosophy to life, was too persistent to be ignored. The opportunity to study Western knowledge was heaven sent. Whether he knew it or not, Ts'ai was on the verge of finding a new perspective for his humanistic yearnings.

14

3

Broadened Horizons

When Ts'ai Yüan-p'ei left Shanghai, he still had in mind the possibility of studying in Europe, and in Peking he explored various government scholarships. The students granted scholarships were being sent to Japan, however, so Ts'ai accepted a position at the Translation Bureau. In 1907, Sun Pao-ch'i (Mu-han), minister-designate of the Chinese government to Germany, offered to assist him to travel to Germany. Ts'ai accepted and joined Sun on the long ride to Berlin.[1] He was also offered a monthly salary by the Commercial Press through his old friend Chang Yüan-chi, in return for occasional articles from Europe.

Ts'ai remained in Berlin for one year, studying the German language, and then attended the University of Leipzig for three years until the outbreak of the revolution in China. While at Leipzig he attended lectures in a wide variety of disciplines, including philosophy, literature, anthropology, comparative culture, and experimental psychology, finally receiving a bachelor of arts degree in 1910.

In addition to his academic studies, Ts'ai wrote extensively and translated a number of works on philosophy, including a *History of Chinese Ethics* [Chung-kuo lün-li-hsüeh-shih], a brief but provocative analysis of traditional ethics in the light of the evolutionary hypothesis. He also translated Friedrich Paulsen's *Principles of Ethics* [Pao-erh-sheng shih lün-li-hsüeh yüan-li] and a primer, *Ethics for the Middle School* [Chung-kuo hsiu-shen chiao-k'o-shu].[2]

Although his four years in Europe took him out of the mainstream of revolutionary politics, it was an important period in his life. Prior to his years in Germany, Ts'ai's intellectual baggage was a motley collection of ideas from China and the West. Significantly, one of his recent interests was Kantian philosophy. He had become acquainted with Kantian idealism in 1903 when he translated Kulpe's *Introduction to Philosophy* into Chinese.[3] Kulpe, a student of Hegel and Kant, had been teaching in Japan, and Ts'ai was impressed with the Kantian attempt to avoid the extremes of idealism and materialism. His reading and study habits would continue during his stay in Europe, although his interest in Kant led him to a deeper interest in modern German philosophy, which eventually provided him with the philosophical basis for a new world view.

For Ts'ai, the most momentous aspect of Western knowledge was the evolutionary hypothesis, which not only destroyed the universalist pretensions of Confucianism, but also laid out guidelines for a new perception of reality based on the conclusions of modern science. Evolutionary theory had not only provided answers to the problems of the modern world, it also asked new questions and raised new controversies, particularly over the moral implications of the evolutionary process. When the Darwinist concept of "survival of the fittest" was applied to human societies, this popularized "social Darwinism" touched a sensitive nerve in Western civilization. By denying the existence of a moral order, social Darwinism had rejected a cardinal tenet of Western thought. Even when Christianity ceased to dominate philosophy in post-Renaissance Europe, Western thinkers accepted the premise that the universe was governed by an ethical as well as a purely cosmic process. Social Darwinism retorted that life was but a grim struggle for survival. In this hostile environment, ethical principles were irrelevant.

Nevertheless, by 1900, social Darwinism became a powerful force in Western thought. It provided a logical justification for the rising tide of Western imperialism washing over Asia and Africa, satisfying the Western need to assure the doubtful that expansion and domination over the East was an inevitable process in civilizing the natives. Social Darwinism had aroused opposition in the West, however, and a number of scientists and philosophers such as Thomas Huxley and John Dewey attempted to alleviate the naturalism of the evolutionary process. A scientifically pretentious attempt to divert evolutionary thought to a more ethically acceptable road was Peter Kropotkin's doctrine of Mutual Aid. Kropotkin had rejected the egoism inherent in social Darwinism by developing the theory of Mutual Aid as the key characteristic of human and subhuman behavior. He insisted that survival took place primarily as a consequence of mutual assistance and relied on scientific evidence to support this phenomenon in the animal kingdom and in the history of the human race. Only in recent centuries had man's natural custom of surviving through tribal and village communities been undermined by individualism in modern society.

Kropotkin believed in the goodness of natural man. In his natural state, man was a rational being, with tendencies for good. Left to his own devices, he would create a society in which Mutual Aid was the primary characteristic of human behavior. The basis for his behavior was not a sense of morality implanted by organized religion, or by the state, or even a devotion to his own pleasures, as hypothesized by the Benthamite utilitarians. A sense of sympathy motivated human action, for the highest pleasure lies in assisting others and in guaranteeing the survival of the human species. State institutions, the Church, the gov-

inequality, prejudice, and destroy man. The state is a coercive instrument, the Church, a tool of the authorities, and private property, an unnatural means which prevents cooperation among men. If governments and other oppressive institutions were abolished, man would return to his natural tendency of cooperating in small communities and would fulfill the utopian goal, "From each according to his abilities, to each according to his needs."[4]

Kropotkin rejected the social foundations of Western civilization and preached revolution as a means of achieving his goal, the overthrow of archaic institutions that prevent man from realizing his dream of a free and peaceful existence. His concept of revolution was as distinctive as his approach to evolution. He admitted, however, that a conscious revolutionary elite would have to awaken the masses to change, using the examples of action, heroism, and self-sacrifice. But Kropotkin denied that in a revolutionary situation a highly disciplined revolutionary authority was necessary. Men will act, he said, when they are free and conscious of their destiny. When they are lethargic, they need to be aroused through education and propaganda. Once aroused, they are capable of a spontaneity of their own. Kropotkin thus not only preached a withering away of the state *after* the achievement of communism, but he rejected the need for a centralized authority during the uprising as well.[5]

The argument over the validity of social Darwinism extended to China where it had an immediate impact on progressive thought. Chinese thought had always attempted to distinguish between the *Wang-tao* and the *Pa-tao*, the "Way of Kings" and the "Way of Force," but the reality of Western behavior in the nineteenth century convinced many Chinese that there was no place for morality in world affairs. They also recognized the importance of power in permitting China to achieve its aims in the world. Acceptance of the primacy of force, however, was not always easy. Wang T'ao asserted that there was still room for virtue in international affairs and that China would restore the primacy of the *Tao* once she had achieved a leading role among modern nations.[6] For Liang Ch'i-ch'ao, the road was somewhat easier. Raised in the Confucian tradition which viewed the universe as fundamentally moral, he yielded to social Darwinism and gradually weaned himself of belief in the primacy of the Way of Kings. By the end of the century, the *Tao* had practically disappeared for him: "In the world there is only power. There is no other force. That the strong always rule the weak is in truth the first great universal rule of nature. Hence, if we wish to attain liberty, there is no other road: we can only seek first to be strong."[7]

Some Chinese continued to be influenced by the Way of Kings and rejected the social Darwinist interpretation of human affairs. Kropotkin's concept of Mutual Aid was the most popular alternative.

Kropotkin's thought entered China through a small group of Chinese in Paris who published a journal, *Hsin shih-chi* [New Century], in the Chinese language devoted to spreading the anarchist ideal throughout Asia.[8] The best-known members of the anarchist group were Wu Chih-hui, Li Shih-tseng, and Chang Ching-chiang.

Ts'ai was introduced to the group through his friend Wu Chih-hui, and they maintained a relationship that lasted for several years; later, the group became known as the Elder Statesmen of the Kuomintang. Kropotkin's theories appealed to Ts'ai Yüan-p'ei for a variety of reasons. Mutual Aid was more congenial to his Confucian training than the cruel naturalism of social Darwinism, yet more scientifically plausible than the primitive *Ta-t'ung* theory that he had liked as a youth. Kropotkin's acceptance of the Communist ideal likewise earned Ts'ai's approbation, as did the anarchist's insistence on the need for mass free action rather than the small revolutionary elite advocated by contemporary Marxists. In its emphasis on the goodness of man in a fundamentally moral universe, but without the oppressive presence of outworn institutions, and in its emphasis on the primacy of ethics over politics in a world characterized by harmony, Mutual Aid coincided with the Confucian humanism of Ts'ai's background, leaving room for a marriage of ethics and modern science. Although Ts'ai was still studying in Germany and did not participate in the journal's activities, he carried away a new view of life which would remain with him long into the future. As a result, Mutual Aid strengthened his opposition to organized religion, militarism, central state authority, and nationalism. It encouraged his belief in humanism, democracy, and mutual co-operation among men. In giving a scientific foundation to the idealism of Ts'ai's youth, Kropotkin's ideas permitted him to focus his attention on social reform and democracy, rather than on its consequences in the world of power.

By accepting the theory of Mutual Aid, Ts'ai rejected the basic premise of many of his nationalist contemporaries, that evolution proceeded primarily through the struggle of man against man, and of society against society. This is not to say that he categorically rejected the trend toward an awakening of the individual and a more vibrant sense of nationhood in China. Far from it, he was about to devote his life to developing a feeling of national identity for the Chinese nation. He was repelled, however, by the image of warring nations as portrayed by the devotees of social Darwinism. When contemporaries such as Yen Fu and Liang Ch'i-ch'ao had concluded that China's historical weakness had been a tendency to pacifism and a lack of the competitive instinct, Ts'ai was anxious to find an alternative which would support a more optimistic view of human nature, and Kropotkin's theory fit his needs.[9] As the Russian anarchist had observed, harmony and cooperation characterized the natural life of man on earth, just as Confucius had maintained so long ago. Thus the Kropotkin interpretation of history could be extended—the process of mutual cooperation operated not only among individuals within a small community, but at the level of intersocietal relations as well. Social progress, Ts'ai contended, was not achieved by a simple weeding out through natural selection of the more primitive societies on earth, but through the process of cultural interchange operating within each social group. The weaker elements in society were not simply eliminated through natural selection; under optimum circumstances they too adapted to new conditions through the elimination of established practices and the importation of new ideas from abroad. Only those societies which isolated themselves from any contact with outside groups were actually weeded out.

As evidence for his contention, Ts'ai often cited the cosmopolitan nature of science and art, both of which transcended national boundaries.[10] This was also true of societies as far apart as China and Europe. European art styles, such as French rococo and Italian Renaissance landscape painting, had been profoundly influenced by Chinese concepts. He began to feel that in the clash of cultures, a form of adjustment took place which was similar to the Golden Mean of Aristotle and the doctrine of the Mean in classical Chinese philosophy. An article entitled "Tendencies toward Harmony Between Eastern and Western Political Ideas" explained his theory:

> These days, living in the world as we are, everything must be viewed as relative, nothing as absolute. . . . The first coming into contact of two distinct ideas invariably brings about a clash, each ridiculing and condemning the other. It is through acquaintance and familiarity that all unconsciously there will result a sort of harmony. Now, it seems, more than ever it is essential to promote mutual understanding of the conceptions of different nationalities and different civilizations. . . . As I have pointed out in a general way, we see now the signs and portents of a harmony between these distinctive political ideas, and there, I believe, lies the hope of Internationalism, for which we all pray and aspire.[11]

The basic problem of modern man, in Ts'ai's view, was not simply modernization, but to learn to live in harmony with his brothers, and to utilize the concept of Mutual Aid instead of the belief that might makes right. History showed that this trend was occurring in the contemporary world. Man was once a savage who loved only himself and those nearest him. Later, through knowledge and understanding, he learned to love others as well. Where primitive man cannibalized and enslaved, modern man realized the ultimate oneness of humanity.[12]

Ts'ai's new philosophy of life was aimed at nationalism, at the growing reliance on force as the determinant of national behavior. Faith in the final victory of internationalism occupied Ts'ai's thoughts, a principle which he would believe in for the remainder of his life. His nationalist-minded colleagues disagreed with him, for in their eyes China needed *more* nationalism, not less. Let other nations practice brotherhood, nationalists stated, then China would happily reciprocate. If there was a growing trend toward harmony in the modern era, let the Western powers be the first to display it.

For Ts'ai, however, belief in Mutual Aid was a matter of faith. Applying his "law of cultural interchange" to the scale of world history, he drew his own conclusions to explain the different rates of advance in China and Europe. In ancient times, Chinese culture was equal to that of the West. Early China began to develop vocations such as agriculture, forestry, labor, and commerce in 2700 B.C., and there were similar beginnings in astronomy, medicine, music, art, and sculpture.[13] By the Chou dynasty, China had become advanced in the natural sciences and philosophy. In all of these respects, it was clearly equal to Western civilization.

Although this similarity continued through the Middle Ages—and Ts'ai had to torture history to equate European scholasticism with Sung Neo-Confucianism—the comparison stopped there. China did not undergo a renaissance and never became a modern society. The answer to the puzzle lay in cultural interchange.[14] In the late medieval period, Europe, profiting from the cultural level of neighboring Arabs and stimulated by contact with Islamic civilization, was encouraged to turn back to the sources of her own Greek and Roman heritage. Out of this contact with a neighboring civilization had grown the Renaissance. China, however, was not so fortunate. With the exception of India, none of her neighbors possessed a cultural level equal to her own. Forced to rely upon her own cultural resources, China had turned inward and had failed to grow after the classical period.

For those conversant with China's history, Ts'ai's interpretation might seem to ignore the influence of Buddhism in China's "middle ages." Had not Buddhism entered China from India during the Han dynasty and brought new points of view which enriched Chinese thought? Ts'ai had trouble with this problem and maintained that the case was not really comparable, since Buddhist concepts of life-negation and opposition to strong family relationships were too exotic in traditional China and, therefore, had exerted little influence. (On the other hand, when dealing with a later period of Chinese history, Ts'ai asserted the evil consequences of Buddhism in China—its influence had prevented the development of natural science, logic, and the separation of politics from religion. Although he could not have it both ways—either Buddhism was an influence or it was not—he did not seem conscious of the contradiction. He could have maintained that Buddhist thought had turned China away from the utilization of her natural energies, a revised version of Yen Fu's viewpoint, which seemed to blame China's stagnation on her ancient sages.)

In any event, we are more concerned with the importance of Ts'ai's historical views than with their weaknesses. The lesson he drew from history was simple and, from his point of view, obvious. Universal truth was not the product of a single culture, but was woven into the fabric of cultures throughout the world. Nations were not like warring savages surviving through the elimination of rivals, but were mutually dependent social organisms which had to cooperate in order to exist. Social and cultural progress was the product of cultural exchange, a pattern which promoted mutual survival and provided a forum for the selection of values and behavior patterns which would encourage the development of mankind. China had mistakenly isolated herself for several centuries, thus denying her people and those of other cultures the opportunity for profitable cultural exchange. Despite her great endowment in human talent and intellect, China had fallen behind other great civilizations in several respects. Now that cultural contact had been resumed after many centuries of disruption, China must make up the lost ground. She need not abandon totally her sense of cultural identity. Indeed, as Ts'ai contended, the total elimination of national and cultural differences was impossible and unwise. As Confucius had said in the *Analects:* "The superior man cultivates harmony, but not sameness."[15] China could achieve progress not by stimulating what Yen Fu considered the natural competitive juices and enlightened self-interest of human beings, but by following a conscious spirit of harmony and love. China need not abandon the Wang-tao in order to obtain the *Ta-t'ung.* Indeed, it was through the Wang-tao that the final utopia could become a reality.

The Final Measure of Value. In advocating a synthesis of values from East and West, Ts'ai was not unique in the general context of his time. Few intellectuals in early twentieth-century China did not foresee that the reform of China would involve a process of borrowing from abroad. But the mere admission of the need to borrow did not end the problem. Basic to the concept of cultural interchange was the question of value. How is the value of a given concept to be established? What will be the ultimate standard of judgment? In the case of ideas artificially imposed from outside, how is the appropriateness of a given concept to be determined within a given culture?

For some, of course, the ultimate judgment of value in early twentieth-century China was the survival and growth of Chinese society. Many probably agreed with Liang Ch'i-ch'ao that force was the only standard in the world, and that the basic law of nature concerned the survival of the stronger. Once that conclusion was accepted, many Chinese felt that value lay in finding the means to make their nation strong enough to compete in a brutal world. In such a world, belief in a spiritual or ethical core to the universe was impossible. Others, while accepting this proposition, felt that some metaphysical foundation was still required, if only as an "opiate for the masses," to serve as a spiritual and ethical basis for behavior until the Chinese people could face a world without a spiritual foundation. It was on this basis that Liang Ch'i-ch'ao and Chang T'ai-yen recommended the continued use of Buddhism.[16] For this reason, K'ang Yu-wei had suggested that Confucianism be made into a religion, pointing out that it was Christianity which had provided the necessary spiritual foundation for Western growth. Although this use of tradition may have been a screen hiding an emotional commitment to traditional values, it was implicit in their attitude that this metaphysical essence would be used for worldly purposes, for the survival and development of the Chinese nation.

After the turn of the century, an increasing number of progressives did not need this particular cultural crutch. Believing in human progress, rationality, and the miracle powers of science so characteristic of the period, many intellectuals came to feel that China did not require a spiritual reality behind the material world, and that science alone would provide a sufficient basis for the moral development of mankind. Not all concluded, however, that a mechanistic universe was necessarily a social Darwinist universe. Some, like the anarchists, followed Kropotkin's optimistic vision of man, and his proposition that man had the keys to work out his salvation on a basis of Mutual Aid.[17] As in Enlightenment Europe, dogmatic theology had been replaced by dogmatic rationalism.

During his years at Leipzig, Ts'ai became aware of the need to base his world view on a sound philosophical basis. Like most modernizers, he wanted a substantial infusion of Western ideas and institutions. As a child of his age, he placed trust in science, in the knowledge obtained through the methods of empirical study, and in the material benefits that modern technology could bestow. But Ts'ai intuitively distrusted an over-reliance on the powers of science and an over-emphasis on the material aspects of human progress which were so strongly stressed by many of his colleagues. The evolution of this strain in his character cannot be traced, although a preoccupation with morality became evident early in his intellectual development. Perhaps with his study of the Neo-Confucianists, he became acutely conscious of the distinction between the material and spiritual aspects of life. In any case, his study of Kant in 1903 deeply impressed him, and when he began his studies in Europe, Ts'ai searched for an ethical and spiritual underpinning to the doctrine of progress in order to combat the trend toward materialism and social Darwinism in the Chinese progressive movement.

By approaching science with a wary though approving eye, Ts'ai differed from Peter Kropotkin, for whose philosophy he had expressed much admiration. Kropotkin had accepted a mechanistic theory of the universe and had felt no need for a metaphysical foundation for his own thought. Anarchism for him was a "world-concept based on a mechanical explanation of all phenomena, embracing the whole of nature; that is, including in it the life of human societies and their economic, political, and moral problems."[18] His aim was "to construct a synthetic philosophy comprehending in one generalization all the phenomena of nature, and therefore also the life of societies." Such conclusions pleased most anarchists in China and many elsewhere in the progressive movement for whom any form of metaphysical reasoning was simply wool-gathering.

Despite his attraction to anarchism and his optimism over the potentialities of science in the modern world, Ts'ai could not accept philosophical materialism as a workable hypothesis of reality. Whether it reflected a traditional repugnance for materialism in the Confucian tradition or his own need for some form of ethico-spiritual core to the universe, he realized that the doctrine of Mutual Aid, rooted in the material world, did not totally satisfy his spiritual needs. There were some questions relating to the nature of man and the universe for which science had no answer. To find these answers, man must turn to religious faith or to philosophy for a deductive hypothesis.[19] The realm of metaphysics, therefore, could not be grasped by human understanding, and each man must search for the answer within himself.

In Germany, where he became more familiar with the thought of the Neo-Kantian movement in Europe, Ts'ai found answers to such problems. His interest in Kant was logical, for the eighteenth-century philosopher had constructed his own system in response to the following trends: the dogmatic theology of the Christian Church and the trend toward dogmatic rationalism in philosophy represented by Leibniz and the empiricists in England. Kant, like Ts'ai, wanted to create a philosophical system which would accept the paramount role of science in the material world, but would also acknowledge the existence of a transcendent moral force in the universe. Kant's solution, of course, was the hypothesis that reality is made up of two parts, the phenomenon and the noumenon, the material everyday world and the spiritual world. In the phenomenal world, science ruled, and knowledge could be attained through human understanding. The noumenal world, however, could not be comprehended through epistemology, but only through metaphysical idealism. By separating knowledge and faith,

Kant had acknowledged the predominance of science in the material world while placing the world of things-in-themselves, the spiritual core of the universe, in a reality all its own which could not be comprehended by the methods of science. Thus man could accept the conclusions of modern science in the material world, but had to rely on personal belief to construct a transcendent spiritual force in the universe.

By separating the realms of knowledge and faith, Kant had opened the door to metaphysical speculation. German philosophy in the mid-nineteenth century began to create grandiose deductive systems pretending to comprehend the ultimate laws of reality—from the idealism of Hegel's "World-Spirit" to the materialistic philosophy of Karl Marx, who "turned Hegel on his head" by putting the speculative historical dialectic to work in an otherwise material universe. For a time, the demarcations between science and faith, originally constructed by Kant, were forgotten. Ultimately, a reaction against deductive philosophy and its opposite, atomistic materialism, set in, and Kantian philosophy achieved a revival at the end of the century. Among such thinkers was the German Neo-Kantian Friedrich Paulsen. Paulsen accepted the division of reality into two parts and rejected the attempts of speculative philosophers to blur the lines between the material world and the metaphysical world, as well as the efforts of materialists to do away with the metaphysical world altogether.

Accepting the importance of science in the phenomenal world, Paulsen attempted to construct a system of metaphysics which would sound scientifically plausible and satisfy the yearnings of humanity for belief in a core of good in the universe. Here he followed the philosophy of Lotze, whose philosophical system accepted the division of the universe into two parts, but saw it as an ultimate unity based on the harmony of all things in a pantheistic all-one. Paulsen followed Lotze in stating that "the reciprocal action and the reign of natural law indicate that the elements of the world are not as unrelated to each other as atomism supposes. The universal connection between all things can be understood by man only on the assumption that they are all parts of a unitary being, of a single substance." This *all-one* was not a transcendent anthropomorphic being, but a law of nature, a world soul, and the source of all individual souls and wills in the universe. Although he admitted that pantheism was not subject to scientific verification, Paulsen claimed to discern an essential unity in all cosmological movements which was the "reflection of an inner harmony, the manifestation of the unified inner life of a spiritual all-one."[20]

Discussing psychical life, Paulsen divided the soul into will and understanding. All living matter possesses a soul life, limited in primitive forms of life to blind volition. In more advanced beings, the soul becomes more self-conscious, until true intelligence, or understanding, appears in human beings. Although individual wills cannot totally comprehend the real world, by understanding the oneness of nature they can obtain a harmony of the myriad individual wills in the universal will of the pantheistic all-one. The world *does* have a design and moral purpose, not provided by an outside anthropomorphic force, but by the interaction of all individual wills united in the universal will.

For Paulsen, as well as Kant, the purpose of constructing a place for metaphysics was to provide a basis for ethics, and Paulsen's philosophy placed a heavy reliance on morality. If Paulsen, like Kant, placed ethics at the heart of his philosophy, he could not accept his colleague's system of ethics in toto. Having been exposed to Darwinist genetic theory, which showed the connection between human behavior and the evolution of society, Paulsen could not accept the formalistic ethics that had been traditional in Christian Europe and had been restated by Kant in philosophical dress. Kant had disagreed with the Church that moral laws could be based on revelation, but he had agreed that morality was a system of pure rational laws, valid a priori and not affected by experience. For Paulsen, ethics could not be separated from the life of society, from history.

At the same time, however, he rejected the nineteenth-century utilitarian pleasure-pain hypothesis. Denying the possibility of a priori judgments in the human mind, the English empirical philosophers concluded that understanding came only from experience and believed that morality could only be enlightened self-interest. This led to utilitarianism, the concept of happiness as the end of morality. To Paulsen, this meant that reason becomes "subservient to the sensuous desires, and denies the possibility of disinterested action."[21] According to him, a value need not measure only immediate sensual pleasure and gratification to be utilitarian. The highest value and pleasure for mankind is the survival of the human race. This goal can best be achieved by man's self-realization, the satisfaction of his spiritual and not merely his bodily needs. This ethic of self-realization, which stresses man's sense of obligation to further the development of life through a realization of his own faculties, provided mankind with the inner moral force necessary to strive for a transcendence of the phenomenal world to a unity with the all-one in the noumenal world. It also replaced the a priori attitude of orthodox Christian morality and Kant's *Critique of Practical Reason,* thus permitting a reconciliation of ethics with evolutionary theory.

Much of Paulsen's philosophy was Kantian, but where Kant's philosophy was rationalistic and formalistic, his was empirical, and took account of the scientific findings of Charles Darwin. Paulsen was influenced, however, by other schools of thought, the pantheism of Lotze and Fechner, Wundt's psychology, and Schopenhauer's doctrine of the will.

Paulsen's philosophy was undoubtedly congenial to Ts'ai because his character resembled the portrait of Paulsen given by William James: "The temper of his mind is essentially ethical, and philosophy for him is nothing if it does not connect itself with active human ideals."[22] Here, of course, Ts'ai had found a kindred spirit. In its recognition of evolutionary historical factors, in its concept of a moral order, and in its acceptance of the scientific interpretation of natural laws, Paulsen's thought also resembled Ts'ai's own views. Here was food for hope, reform, progress, and man's duty to society. Like Confucianism, Paulsen believed that man must cultivate himself and serve society. Certainly Paulsen's attempt to synthesize opposing currents of thought struck a responsive chord in Ts'ai's penchant for moderation and compromise. We shall be observing other Western influences on the philosophical thought of Ts'ai Yüan-p'ei, although none will alter his basic views, formed through his association with Neo-Kantianism in Germany. He expressed admiration for other philosophical systems, such as Comte's positivism and the vitalism of Bergson, but it was Paulsenianism which truly influenced his philosophical thought.

Although Ts'ai never pretended that his philosophical ideas possessed great originality, he was convinced that they formed an appropriate philosophical basis for his world view. After the revolution of 1911, Ts'ai returned to China to become the minister of education in the new Republic. At this time, he was under the influence of Neo-Kantian views on cosmology and ontology, and his actions and public statements reflected a desire to popularize his system in China. His first major proposed reforms in education presented in 1912 were based on Paulsen's concepts, and that year he also published an article in the journal *Eastern Miscellany* [Tung-fang tsa-chih] in which he outlined his world view.[23] Ts'ai's philosophical thoughts are scattered throughout his works, but the locus of his ideas is a primer on philosophy written in Europe in 1913 and published in China in 1916. Ostensibly a survey of modern trends in European philosophy, Ts'ai made a number of editorial comments which clearly indicated his own views. After that point, he devoted less attention to the propagation of his views on metaphysics and concentrated on social and educational reform. This does not reflect a decline in his convictions, although he probably realized that theory, as divorced from practice, had little appeal to the reform generation then maturing in China. Ts'ai would henceforth deal with practical problems, but his solutions would continue to reflect the beliefs he had acquired in Germany.

The foundation of Ts'ai's ontology is the Kantian (and Paulsenian) division of reality between the phenomenal [*hsien-hsiang*] and the noumenal [*shih-t'i*] world. He viewed the phenomenal world as relative, empirical, and irrevocably tied to time and space, while the noumenal world is absolute, intuitive, and not subject to temporal or spatial limitations. Like Kant and Paulsen, Ts'ai took the idealist view that neither empirical nor rational methods would suffice to permit an absolute knowledge of reality.[24] Like Paulsen, he did not assign precedent in obtaining relative knowledge to either empirical or rational methods. Ordinary knowledge, he believed, was a product of both processes. Reality itself was made up of spirit and matter, two sides of one reality.

For the connecting links in the universe, Ts'ai followed Paulsen into pantheism. God, or the law of nature, was not a transcendent being, but the deepest and original fount of the earth. The all-one was a world soul and the source of all individual souls and wills in the universe. He followed Fechner through Paulsen in hypothesizing animation or soul-life (will) in animal and inorganic life; all souls were therefore part of the world soul. Like Paulsen, Ts'ai admitted that idealistic pantheism was only a theory, but contended that it had the fewest weaknesses of all cosmological theories in existence. For those questions which science cannot answer, Ts'ai believed, each man must find his own solution in religion or philosophy. Ts'ai found his in Paulsen. In 1912, Ts'ai wrote the following about the world soul:

> It is impossible to give it a name. But it is necessary to give it a name in order that it can become a concept, and therefore it can be called the Way [*Tao*] or the Supreme Ultimate [*T'ai-chi*], the Spirit [*Shen*], the Power of Darkness [*Hei-an chih i-shih*] or even the Blind Will [*Wu-shih chih i-chih*]. It can be given a thousand names, but there exists but one concept.[25]

Thus the world soul found its manifestation in all cultures, the Jehovah of the Jews, the Buddha of Asia, the World Spirit of Hegel, and the deities of primitive animism.

Religion and Aesthetics. Since Ts'ai's views on the nature of reality were merely a reflection of the philosophical ideas he acquired in Europe, they have little interest to us beyond their indication of the general orientation of his philosophical thought. What is more distinctive is the way he attempted to link the spiritual world to that of man, the application of his philosophical views to his reformist impulse. Paulsen had justified belief in the existence of a moral universe —a world of harmony and goodness—rather than the harsh world posited by social Darwinism, and he had concluded that Christianity would be the instrument to move mankind toward his goal. Here Ts'ai differed from his German mentor, for, unlike Paulsen, he did not see organized religion as a means of developing man's sense of brotherly love and the spiritual sense. Ts'ai even maintained that religion was a divisive force in society, inciting man to build walls of local prejudice and superstition, discouraging him from the unfettered search for knowledge.[26]

In attempting to free man from his dependence on religion, Ts'ai placed primary reliance on education. If traditional man saw religion as the instrument to teach brotherly love and provide knowledge of the natural world, Ts'ai conceived of education as fulfilling analogous goals. The ultimate goal of society was to transcend the phenomenal world and attain harmony with the universal will in the noumenal world, "to combine all beings in a harmonious whole where mutual differences have disappeared."[27] Since the noumenal world was not located beyond the material world, but within it, the key to achieving this transformation would be found by improving the conditions of human life on earth. Through the advancement of knowledge, man could eliminate ignorance, prejudice, poverty, and disease. Knowledge of other cultures would increase human sympathy and understanding, enabling man to comprehend the oneness of all living things.

But knowledge alone would not suffice to end human misery and conflict. Man had to cease thinking in terms of self-benefit in order to develop a disinterested world view, filled with a love of all living things. Fearing that listeners would equate his philosophy with Buddhism in its rejection of human desires, Ts'ai emphasized that a nihilistic rejection of the world was not a proper attitude. On the contrary, man had to strive to improve the world around him. But Ts'ai agreed with Buddhism that dependence on the material aspects of life should be avoided, and that "one should cultivate a longing for the realization of the noumenal world, and a gradual apprehension of this world. The principles of free speech should be advocated, and philosophical factionalism should be avoided, with no ideological dogmatism to blind the heart, in order that an objective, limitless world outlook can be created."[28]

Attempting to transcend the material world and find an understanding of the real world beyond, Ts'ai turned to aesthetics. His use of aesthetics in this case is reminiscent of the Confucian emphasis on music as a means of cultivating the superior man. More influential in forming his views, however, was Kantian philosophy, which stressed the universal nature of the appreciation of beauty and its capacity to provide a feeling of emotional detachment. While studying in Germany, Ts'ai realized that aesthetics could be the connecting link between the noumenal and the phenomenal world, and if scientific knowledge could dispel the obstacles to harmony in the phenomenal world, art could describe the nature of the real world and raise its understanding in human society. In the appreciation of beauty, the emotions of the phenomenal world, love and hate, sadness and joy, are transferred to the object of contemplation, and only an understanding of beauty remains. Ts'ai used the example of a volcanic eruption, which inspires awe and fear in real life, but only a detached feeling of beauty in a painting.[29] Because the appreciation of beauty is universal and does not distinguish between the self and the nonself, it is able to subdue the desire to possess that which is characteristic of behavior in the material world. Aesthetics education, therefore, enables man to overcome the psychological obstacles and reach the noumenal world. The appreciation of beauty by mankind, having reduced prejudice, greed, ignorance, and superstition, could transform the world into one harmonious family.

Ts'ai's theories on metaphysics are partly typical of the times, and partly distinctive. In their use of Western science and rejection of orthodox religion, they reflect the basic trends of the age. On the other hand, he was probably unique in China for having combined political radicalism with a system of philosophical idealism. He obviously saw the spiritual sense as useful in forwarding man's goals on earth. There is no hint, however, that his metaphysical theories were meant as an "opiate for the masses" to be turned on and off at will. Why didn't a native theory serve his needs? He was personally attracted to Taoism in which he found three benefits: its similarity to modern socialism, its encouragement to man to work for an understanding of the real world beyond the material phenomena of nature, and its advocacy of indifference to death and misery in this life. By its rejection of action, however, Taoism contrasted greatly with the doctrine of progress, and thus could only prosper in chaotic times.

Buddhism and Taoism, in essence, were too passive for Ts'ai's positivist sensibilities. He was highly conscious of the suffering which desire caused in the material world. But unlike the Buddhists, he did not advocate the elimination of desire through a total rejection of the phenomenal world. The material world, after all, is not an illusion, but the framework in which man must operate. Desire can be eliminated only through an understanding of man's role in the world, and of the real world within. In this respect, the role of man's knowledge of the world and of himself would be paramount.

Ts'ai realized that there was an ultimate subjective foundation underlying his empirical superstructure. He had accepted the Neo-Kantian view that final knowledge of reality could not be attained and that the ultimate decision on the choice of a metaphysical belief was based on human will, the Kantian leap of faith. Even here, he tried to escape subjectivism by claiming that pantheism was the most logical answer to scientific questions regarding the nature of life and the universe.[30] He was confident that pantheism would be the religion of the future, fulfilling its role in the search for answers to cosmological questions. He cited the growth of theosophical societies in the West, which abandoned ritual and prayer and replaced them with literature and art, synthesizing the spiritual core of all the religions and philosophies of man.

Ts'ai's belief in monistic pantheism was an essential element in his philosophy, since he felt that this metaphysical reality supported belief in an organic unity to mankind and the universe as a whole. The transcendence of the material world to the real world by all mankind would signal, therefore, the approach of utopia on earth. And here Ts'ai's metaphysics joined his theories on social reform. The means of achieving this unity in the universal all-one was through the elimination of poverty, ignorance, and disease. Since the noumenal world was located within the material world, the achievement of unity would have to be realized here, not in a transcendent world to come. For Ts'ai, therefore, the reduction of human conflict and misery in the material world would lead to the harmonization of human wills.

Ts'ai had gone a long way from the simple three desires of the obscure *Shao-hsing Chih-hsueh-hui*. The new structure demanded an optimistic attitude about the law of nature and the future of the human race, a staunch trust in knowledge which would drive from mankind poverty, ignorance, and prejudice. In particular, it required confidence in the human intellect. In Europe, Kant had liberated man from the limitations of Hume's empiricism. Thought now governed spiritual reality, and the mind no longer had to accommodate itself to nature, but the other way around. Ts'ai accepted the responsibility Kant had offered and had postulated a reality that satisfied his own needs. He avoided a dogmatic approach to reality, however, and insisted that men must have freedom to formulate their own understanding of the nature of the universe. He was confident that man would be satisfied with neither a mechanical theory of the universe nor with religious dogma.

Ts'ai's philosophical ideas seemed to blend the Confucian emphasis on order and harmony with the Western belief in change and progress. Science was paramount in explaining the laws of the phenomenal world, but could not explain events in the noumenal world. For that, man must turn to philosophy.[31] But science should do its best to expose philosophy to empirical analysis. And all metaphysical theories, from Buddhism to the Bergsonian *Elan Vital,* were welcome as a supplement to modern scientific knowledge. For himself, however, Ts'ai posited a reality which corresponded to his own predilections—a universe characterized by order and harmony, a vision of man endowed with rationality and the capacity to resolve the problems of human society. If Confucianism was to be left behind, there was yet a distinct resemblance to Confucius in his own philosophy.

Ethics for a New Age. Convinced that the resolution of the problems of mankind was dependent on the betterment of man himself, that social reform had to be accompanied by the enlightenment of the population in order to be effective, it is hardly surprising that ethics was at the center of Ts'ai's thought. For ethics is the connecting link between philosophical theory and social practice, the spiritual beyond and the materialist here and now. The ultimate success of a philosophy of life involving a recognition of the free will of man would depend on the moral and intellectual level of man himself. This would be true in the case of Ts'ai's world view in which the elevation of the moral qualities of humanity played an important role.

By concentrating on the problems of ethics, Ts'ai showed a resemblance to Confucius himself, for the core of Confucian philosophy had been its code of human behavior. For Confucius, as for Ts'ai, metaphysics was a backdrop for the main concern, the construction of the good society on earth. Although Ts'ai must have been indebted to Confucius, the modern reformer realized the need for a marked departure from many traditional Confucian norms. Ts'ai did not attack Confucian ethics with the visible contempt of a Tsou Jung, who portrayed traditional values as those of a slave mentality. Ts'ai attempted to judge Confucian ethics with an evolutionary *coup d'oeil,* to place traditional thought in its historical perspective while showing the irrelevance of these values in the modern world. Confucianism had been a natural outgrowth of ancient family society and was not appropriate to modern China.[32]

Ts'ai's feelings reflected the negative attitude Chinese intellectuals were developing toward traditional values. There was general agreement in the progressive movement that one of China's primary needs was a new code of behavior. The utility of the evolutionary hypothesis in this context is apparent. Once ethics was seen in an evolutionary setting, there was nothing to hold back the historico-genetic concept that man's idea of behavior evolves with his social and psychological needs. That gave the reformers the opportunity to construct a new system of morality based on modern needs. Resembling Europe as it experienced the decay of the formalistic standards of medieval Christendom, Chinese reformers found that utility showed the best promise for the ultimate standard of judgment.

What, in the eyes of the reform generation, was wrong with traditional ethics? For advocates of democracy, of course, the subordination of the individual was at variance with the Western ethic—with its stress on freedom and self-realization. Perhaps the main concern for most modernizers was the Chinese lack of energy and a supine acceptance of fate. Symptomatic of this problem was the indifference of the Chinese people to the humiliation of their nation by foreigners. Traditional morality, which emphasized family loyalty instead of the individual's responsibility to his nation, had oriented the people toward local problems only, and this was an obstacle to the transformation of China into a strong and united nation. This concern had been expressed by many reformers, but it had been best expressed by Liang Ch'i-ch'ao, as he attempted to formulate a new morality for the Chinese people. Liang, borrowing ideas from Yen Fu, advocated the creation of new ethics based on public, not private morality.[33] The beam in Liang's eye was the distressing habit of the Chinese to direct their loyalty to the family and the clan, rather than to the nation. The aim of his New Morality was to transfer this loyalty to the nation. At that time, however, Liang was not moving as far away from Confucian tradition as he might have thought. Although he had his eye on Western values as he formulated his ideas, he was not arguing for the adoption of individualism. Indeed, he opposed individualism as characteristic of a barbarian age [ye-man shih-tai]. Distrustful of the rationality of the individual, Liang wanted group freedom, the subordination of the individual to the nation, rather than to the family. Like Hegel, Liang found freedom in the concept of the nation-state. Although there was a tendency in the revolutionary movement to view with approval the Western concept of individual freedom, even Sun Yat-sen shared Liang's distrust of liberty in a Chinese context. Sun was equally insistent on the priority of national over individual goals and was willing to rely on the traditional concepts of loyalty [chung] and filial piety [hsiao] to obtain national unity and purpose.

Ts'ai had agreed with Liang in criticizing the traditional localism of the Chinese people. In his story "Dream of a New Year," he had railed at the unconcern of the villager for Russian aggression in the North and had indicated that before China could become a great nation, her citizens would have to give their loyalty to the national unit. When Ts'ai was directly exposed to Western values, however, he parted ways with his famous contemporary. He did not share Liang's distrust of the individual. Given his emphasis on the individual's role in the development of human progress, he could hardly do so. Ts'ai was not anxious to free the individual from all obligations to serve the community. Nor could he place primary loyalty in the concept of the nation-state, as Liang had done. For Ts'ai, the nation was only a transitional stage to the internationalism of the ultimate utopia. This attitude had already appeared in "Dream of a New Year," when he had asserted that the formation of a strong nation was only a stage to the final harmony of all mankind.[34]

The key problem in ethics, then, was to reconcile individual needs with the community good. From Ts'ai's point of view, man's freedom had to be affirmed, and at the same time his moral obligation to the community was stressed. It was in Europe that he found the vehicle for the expression of his ideas. Ts'ai's exposure to evolutionary thought had made him a convert to ethical utilitarianism, probably since his early revolutionary days. In Europe, however, he became attracted to anarchist ethics, then to the brand of utilitarianism advocated by Friedrich Paulsen, which attempted to avoid the pitfalls of pure hedonism and a priori formalism. Ts'ai accepted utility as the ultimate standard of judgment, that behavior had to be judged in terms of its results. His high hopes for humanity, however, caused him to reject the hypothesis that man is motivated by purely selfish aims. Nor could he accept the implications of hedonistic [li-chi] pleasure-pain utilitarianism, which stressed man's basic drives for personal happiness, long life, and power. Such motives did not conform to his ideal of Mutual Aid. Ts'ai built his own ethical system on the foundation of Paulsen's teleological energism. (It might also be said that his ethical views were borrowed from Kropotkin, since there is similarity between the systems advocated by the German Neo-Kantian and the Russian revolutionary. When discussing ethics, however, Ts'ai usually used terminology reminiscent of Paulsen's teleological energism. Therefore, it is reasonable to assume that Paulsen's ethics, rather than Kropotkin's, formed the basis of Ts'ai's beliefs.) According to Paulsen, man's goals were not only personal happiness and pleasure, but self-realization [tzu-ch'eng], the fulfillment of the objective content of life. Ts'ai agreed with Paulsen that "analytical psychology is wrong in holding that the idea of pleasure is the constant motive of human volition. The goal at which the will aims does not consist in a maximum of pleasurable feelings, but in the normal exercise of the vital functions for which the species is predisposed. The will strives for an objective content of life, and the type of life becomes a conscious ideal of life."[35] Reaching for an example, Ts'ai cited the fact that parents always plan for the well-being of their children and grandchildren, even at their own expense. But the concern of mankind is not limited to the family, since men are also willing to sacrifice themselves for national survival. Nevertheless, nationalism is insufficient. In an article written in 1912, Ts'ai directly attacked advocates of national wealth and power:

> Those who misread evolution say that the main goal of mankind is simply the survival of the self and the race, and therefore promote the idea of might makes right as the highest morality. . . . But if you make racial survival the highest aim, then the greatest virtue must necessarily be maintenance of the purity of the race. But pure races which prohibit intermarriage are seldom prosperous, while the great civilizations of ancient and modern times have always been racially mixed. . . . So what kind of an aim is that?[36]

Self-realization lies in furthering the happiness and progress of all humanity. Since man must die and nations must decay, "if all the people of a nation pass from generation to generation a goal of life happiness which is extinguishable by death, then what is the value of man on earth? If this is the meaning of life . . . then what is the meaning of sacrifice to achieve human-heartedness [*jen*], of the sacrifice of one's life for righteousness [*i*], of sacrifice of the self for humanity?"[37] If that were the case, he concluded, men would have no adventurous spirit and would not attempt long-term planning. All activity would be directed at immediate personal benefit. To satisfy his need for self-realization, man must have a goal that transcends his own interests.

Ts'ai added that self-realization and willingness to sacrifice did not mean pure altruism. While selflessness is admirable, he saw little scope for it in the contemporary world. In seeking self-realization, man compromises his desire for individual happiness with the broader needs of humanity. When a conflict between the two arises, then he must sacrifice his own interests.[38] Through self-realization, all the individual wills in the world are eventually expanded into a common will, so that man can achieve happiness in society as well as understand the nature of the real world. This harmony of wills in the spiritual all-one involves more than humanity itself. It includes all life which possesses a consciousness of joy and sorrow: animals, as well as organic and inorganic matter. The highest value, therefore, transcends not only the self and the nation, but humanity as well.

Here Ts'ai has approached a moral concern for all living beings more closely associated with Indian religious thought than the practical Chinese. He was aware that perfect adherence to this ideal was impossible to achieve. He himself abstained from eating meat until advised otherwise by a doctor. He readily ate vegetables, explaining that in decisions of this nature man had to judge the moral alternatives.[39] He tended to discuss these issues on a philosophical plane, and rarely discussed or wrote about the panpsychic aspects of his thought. Perhaps he felt that an enlightenment of the masses at this level would be impossible until the educational groundwork had been carefully laid.

Ts'ai's opposition to hedonism brings up an interesting comparison with the philosophical issue discussed by Professor Benjamin Schwartz in his study of Yen Fu—the relation of the cosmic process to that of ethics.[40] Like Spencer, Yen saw ethical values as an intrinsic part of the cosmic process. The evolutionary law of natural selection creates in man the need for security. In his struggle for survival, man sees the value of mutual sympathy; therefore "enlightened self-interest" calls for the cooperation of men in a community. Behind this self-interest, however, lies a hedonistic concern for the self, and only a secondary one for the survival of others. Morality is the means, personal survival the end—this process was built into the cosmic law of evolution. Thomas Huxley, an evolutionist, but an opponent of social Darwinism, had retorted that there was no ethical strain in the law of nature. By his "horticultural instinct," man himself provided moral values in order to alleviate the cruel naturalism of the universe. Mutual sympathy, the basis of morality, was not found in the cosmic process, but was created in the mind of man.

Whether Ts'ai was aware of the controversy in Europe, or of Yen Fu's approach to it, is unknown. In any case, his own assessment of morality falls between the positions held by Spencer and Huxley. Like Spencer and Yen Fu, he believed that the cosmic process embraced the ethical one. In his monistic universe, there had to be a place for the moral sense. But he could not see the final justification of moral behavior in anything so hedonistic as "enlightened self-interest." Mutual sympathy is at the heart of man. He does not, of course, neglect his own needs, but he is able to see the broader perspective of humanity that is beyond himself. This sense of oneness is not highly developed in lower organisms, but becomes evident as evolution progresses. At its higher levels, man is willing to sacrifice himself for the good of the community. Teleological energism, not enlightened self-interest, is the key to the moral urge. By acknowledging man's instinct to further the survival of the species, Ts'ai had followed the position taken by Huxley (and by Peter Kropotkin). By following Paulsen into monistic pantheism, however, he maintained that this instinct is part of the cosmic process.

The difference between enlightened self-interest and teleological energism may not seem great, since Spencer's enlightened hedonist would probably accept the survival of his community and his species as essential to his own well-being. Yet Yen Fu and Ts'ai were led in different directions. Yen followed enlightened self-interest into history and contemporary politics, finding self-assertion and the concerns for personal and national power both natural and moral. After all, this quality had made the West great and would have the same effect in China. Ts'ai, on the other hand, followed teleological energism through Mutual Aid to a vision of life in which a muting of individual desires is the key to progress and happiness. Yen's self-assertion would find expression in the nation-state, Ts'ai's self-realization was aimed at dissolving the artificial distinctions among mankind.

Whether the individual would sacrifice his interests to the good of the larger community was at the root of the problem. According to Ts'ai, the individual would see that his interests and the needs of the community would naturally coincide, and that there was a natural "harmony of interests" between the rights of man and the good of society. This had been the proposition stated by the *philosophes* of the European Enlightenment, in the fullness of their optimism over the potential goodness of natural man. As E. H. Carr has pointed out, the concept of the "harmony of interests" began to break down in nineteenth-century Europe under the pressure of economic competition and the rise of imperialism, giving way to the concept of social Darwinism, by which it was conceded that the loser in the struggle for survival might be physically eliminated from competition. Ts'ai Yüan-p'ei and other anarchists intended to redress this breakdown by demonstrating that the hedonism of contemporary social practice was a product not of the natural tendencies of man, but of the modern social institutions which he has constructed.

Teleological energism became a basic theme for Ts'ai in articles and speeches throughout his public life. Like the Victorian Samuel Smiles, he published a book of moral platitudes to provide a moral uplift for the common man. The titles indicate the nature of the morality: "Exert effort for the public benefit," "Sacrifice yourself for the group," "Pay attention to public health," "Don't do unto others what you would not want done unto you," "Judge yourself severely and others lightly," and "Love animals."[41] Whether Ts'ai's essays were widely read in China is doubtful, but they were distributed among Chinese studying and working in Europe during the First World War.

When discussing individual morality, Ts'ai stressed man's obligation to serve society, to serve the future rather than the present, and to search for spiritual pleasure rather than bodily enjoyment. To indicate the familiarity of his concepts, he often quoted Confucius: "That which you yourself desire, do for others, and that which you wish to happen to yourself, make happen to others" [chi yü li erh li jen, chi yü ta erh ta jen].

In an essay "Sacrifice yourself for the group" [She-chi wei ch'ün], he claimed that the group is more important than the individual, and whenever a conflict of interest occurs, the individual should sacrifice his goals for the needs of the group. This is justified on the grounds that the individual cannot survive without the group, whereas the group does not need the individual. In the light of this position, it is understandable that he rated man's obligations as greater than his privileges. The individual must provide for the continued existence of society, and the privileges he receives from society are in the nature of fuel to encourage him to fulfill his social obligations. Even Confucius agreed: "In life no one is idle."[42]

Such hypotheses, of course, would be of little use if mankind lived in a social Darwinist world of sheer survival of the stronger. The whole structure demands acceptance of Ts'ai's basic hypotheses, of monistic pantheism, Mutual Aid, and the perfectibility of man. Such premises must ultimately be based on will, since there can be no final knowledge of reality. That there was a rational and ethical order to the universe was Ts'ai's gamble.

In his vision of ethics and society, Ts'ai was preserving much of the essence of Confucian morality while abandoning its externals. Both systems approached the problem of man's role in society with the same presumption, that a good society could be constructed only if the individual were willing to sacrifice his interest to that of the community. More specifically, Ts'ai reflected that aspect of the Confucian tradition which stressed concern for the individual and voluntarism. Actually, his philosophical thought is a modern variation of the Mencian concept of the *Wang tao*, a reliance on the goodness of the individual in promoting the welfare of society, and a fervent belief in the existence of a moral order. Although he criticized many aspects of traditional morality, Ts'ai maintained great respect for the fundamental Confucian virtues. Indeed, as he would later state, the new morality that he was promoting did not negate traditional morality, but went beyond it.

Problems of Synthesis and Commitment. As a result of his years of study in Europe, Ts'ai Yüan-p'ei had begun to stake out a humanist approach to the problems of building a new society—a view that already contrasted with the nationalist emphasis displayed by many of his contemporaries. Although he shared the desire of his radical comrades to overthrow the Manchu dynasty and instill a sense of patriotism in the minds of the Chinese people, Ts'ai's aims had already begun to diverge from the mainstream. In adopting the ideas of Kropotkin and Paulsen, it seems that Ts'ai had strengthened inclinations already evident in his early maturity. The tenor of his thought from our earliest indications was humanist and ethical, with an inclination toward the search for ultimate goals for all mankind. The premises that supported his philosophical scheme—the existence of a moral order and the perfectibility of man—were likewise rooted in his early experience, although at a more intuitive level. His years of European study did not change his orientation toward ethics, but helped him to formulate an all-inclusive scheme to replace the obsolescent Confucian hypothesis. In many respects, the continuity of his thought from his early exposure to Neo-Confucianism to the years in Leipzig is striking.

This does not mean, of course, that the influence of Western philosophy on his thought was superficial. It demonstrates, however, as Benjamin Schwartz showed in his study on Yen Fu, that a Chinese intellectual caught in the web between East and West would mold his borrowings from abroad into a shape designed to fit his own perception of Chinese society. These adjustments are not lacking in Ts'ai Yüan-p'ei's philosophical system. In his metaphysics, he accepted the Neo-Kantian division between reason and faith, but not for the purpose of providing a justification for the practice of organized religion. Like many Chinese intellectuals, Ts'ai had no need for religion in its narrow sense and utilized Kantian idealism for the sole purpose of positing an ethical core to the universe. In the realm of ethics, he placed greater reliance on community service than Paulsen or his predecessor. Kantian ethics was preoccupied with the individual and the problems of determining the basis for ethical behavior. Ts'ai Yüan-p'ei did not ignore such problems, but attempted to justify the Confucian emphasis on harmony and the subordination of the individual to society. Kant's concern for the individual was shifted to reflect a Chinese intellectual's concern for the destiny of the community as a whole.

One of the most striking aspects of Ts'ai's thought is the degree to which he relied on the concept of *value* in choosing ideas for cultural reform. He was an exponent of the view that value is where you find it, an advocate, in the words of the late Joseph R. Levenson, of "the best in East and West."[43] This is not to say that he was not conscious of the problem of rapid change. Though an advocate of change, he believed that reforms must be gradual to be effective.

Occasionally, he tried to provide guidelines which would help China reform at a safe rate of acceleration. Once he used the analogy of the human digestive system. Human cultures must absorb and digest like the organs of the human body. China must be willing not only to absorb [*hsi-shou*] foreign influences, but to digest [*hsiao-hua*] them as well.[44] A long period of digestion, rather than one of forced feeding, must take place to diminish the problems caused by absorption. As for the extent of change, he continued using the example of the digestive system. In absorption, he said, you do not swallow everything; the bones and seeds must be rejected, or digestive problems will occur. To give historical depth to his argument, Ts'ai referred to Buddhism, which had never been digested in China and whose reliance on superstition continued to pose an obstacle to the evolution of Chinese society. China, then, should avoid swallowing the bones and seeds of Western civilization—its political instability, its greed, and its religious intolerance—and absorb only those elements which would aid her growth.

By the same token, the absorption of Western ideas did not imply the total abandonment of the national heritage. On countless occasions, he pointed out the similarity of Western ideas to traditional Chinese ones. In the past, China had developed many of the political, social, and cultural values now necessary to create a new China. In many instances, she had abandoned these values. Since she had discovered them once, however, she could certainly use them again. What was new and unfamiliar to Chinese today was not necessarily alien to their whole tradition. Consequently, Confucian thought need not be wholly discarded. Indeed, it shared many qualities with modern concepts advocated by the American educator John Dewey, such as the emphasis on individual character and the value of learning and experience. Confucius differed from Dewey, however, in his acceptance of male superiority and devotion to the principle of monarchy, points of view which reflected the gap in time and knowledge. A cautious middle course would result in the growth of Chinese society, not only in science, and in the revitalization of art and culture, but in the quality of life as well, in food, clothing, housing, and education.[45] Emotional rejection or an uncritical acceptance of the West were therefore equally mistaken.

To one observer, Ts'ai's attempt to avoid emotional commitment by advocating reform on the basis of *value* (those ideas and institutions most appropriate to China, regardless of their country of origin), rather than *history* (the values and institutions of the Chinese cultural heritage) was only partly successful. According to Joseph Levenson, Ts'ai's concept of "the best in East and West" was, in reality, "a balm for cultural defeatism" since, in effect, he was asking the West to recognize the values found in Chinese culture as China had already recognized those of the West.[46] The fact that Ts'ai believed in the value of Chinese culture, as well as Western, meant that there was value to be found in both. In reality, however, the West had found very little in China to aid her own cultural development. In his attempt to transcend the demands of *history* to find a universal world of *value*, Ts'ai was attempting to disarm *history* so that no one would feel deprived at the irrelevance of his native values, since values are universal in any case.

This is an astute observation, and may be true in the case of many Chinese intellectuals attempting to square their emotional commitment to China with their rational belief in the necessity for reform along Western lines.[47] But I do not believe this contention is justified in the case of Ts'ai's attitude, at least during the prerevolutionary period. To deny that he lacked a sense of pride in Chinese culture and would happily point to areas where China had achieved a level of cultural sophistication comparable to the West would be senseless. His motive in developing the concept of a synthesis of values was not cultural equivalence, but the concepts of Mutual Aid and cultural interchange.

Ts'ai's emotional commitment to Mutual Aid is clearly revealed in his writings on the comparative history of Eastern and Western civilizations. In these articles, Ts'ai often went to considerable pains to show the parallel between the cultural achievement of Chou China and classical Greece. China, he maintained, was in every important respect the equal of Europe during the classical phase of development.[48] Then, he continued, China went into a period of cultural isolation from which she is only now emerging, while Europe, after a period of stagnation, revived her evolutionary advances during the Renaissance and built the foundations of modern Western civilization. Here again, we find nothing exceptionable. Ts'ai has effectively conceded that China today is not equal to the West. This inequality, at least implicitly, is spiritual as well as material, since evolution in his eyes involves progress in both fields.

Ts'ai did not lead us here solely to demonstrate that China had her logic and mathematics, to beg that Westerners look with admiration at Mo Tzu and Chuang Tzu as they have always respected Aristotle and Socrates. It is now, however, that he is anxious to make his point: why did Europe revive while China did not? Europeans survived because they broke out of their self-imposed isolation, imported the advanced culture of Arabia, and, stimulated by this cultural transfusion, turned back to the sources of their own early greatness in Greece and Rome and began a modern revival. Ts'ai is straining here to prove his point. Few students of the Renaissance would claim that it was Arabian culture *per se* which sparked the European revival. It helped to preserve the classical knowledge of Greece, perhaps, but Arabic culture hardly exerted a decisive influence on the evolution of European society. There is another criticism of Ts'ai's historical rambling—his disposal of Buddhism as a factor in Chinese development. He has asserted that it was too negative to exert any influence on China, yet he does not demonstrate the positive qualities of Arabic culture which had a stimulating effect on Europe.

Why has Ts'ai been forced to twist history? Obviously, he has tried to provide convincing historical evidence for his faith in the magic qualities of cultural interchange, of Mutual Aid as the key to the evolutionary process. In advocating "value where you find it," Ts'ai is not trying to convince the West to borrow from China, or to establish Chinese equivalence with the West, but to provide historical evidence for his own philosophy of evolution. He is guilty, therefore, of letting emotion intrude on his judgment, but his emotional claim is not to *history* but to the concept of Mutual Aid. He has committed himself to a theory of historical development which became an essential cornerstone of his philosophy of reform; and to that end all else, even Chinese culture, had to be sacrificed.

No doubt, some used the idea of "the best in East and West" to satisfy the claims of history. If the defense of tradition by moderates, however, was a cover for a need to preserve familiar values in a strange new world, we are not necessarily justified in viewing this as a victory of emotion over rationality. By hindsight, we know that gradualism and the synthetic approach failed in early twentieth-century China. At the time, however, a policy of gradual reform, combining the new with the familiar, seemed as logical as total and immediate Westernization, as advocated by the revolutionaries.[49] Although Chinese synthesizers may have been unaware of it at the time, the evidence of modern social science was already suggesting that a radical break with tradition could cause emotional dislocation and loss of identity in society—and consequently result in slower progress than might have been achieved by gradualism. The reader need not accept the truth of this assertion to concede that it could exert a persuasive force on the mind of a Chinese intellectual lost in the labyrinth of late Manchu society. When the progressive Chinese intellectuals chose to sprinkle their writings with quotations from the ancients, to find Chinese equivalents for Western ideas, they were not necessarily attempting to satisfy a personal need to establish Chinese equivalence, but to demonstrate to their audiences that the Western reforms they were advocating had roots in Chinese civilization, to domesticate them to an Asian environment.

In any event, Ts'ai was launched on a course that would make him one of the most prominent advocates of humanism in twentieth-century China. For the time being, the moment was propitious. China was about to enter a period in which humanist values would receive warm support from progressive intellectuals and did not seem to contradict the primordial goals of nationalism. From our perspective in history, the circumstances were not as auspicious as they may have seemed at the time. Western imperialism had turned East Asia into a laboratory for social Darwinism, and it is not surprising that most Chinese would come to see life as a grim struggle for national and personal survival. Ts'ai simply could not accept these conclusions and was prepared to devote the rest of his life to disprove them.

4

Minister of Education

In 1911, after more than a decade of sporadic attempts at revolution, the old dynasty was overthrown. The revolutionaries were now able to undertake their program of reform. The two immediate beneficiaries were the exiled revolutionary Sun Yat-sen, whose revolutionary organization, soon to be reorganized into the legal *Kuomintang* party, formed a provisional government under his leadership in Nankirg, and the military leader Yüan Shih-k'ai, who had succeeded through stratagem to a position of power in Peking.

Ts'ai, now forty-three years of age, was still in Germany when revolution broke out. He had not been active in the revolutionary movement since 1906, but had maintained his contacts with many of the revolutionary leaders. After the outbreak of the revolt, he went to Berlin where he discussed the situation with students, sending suggestions to the rebels through his friend Wu Chih-hui, and awaiting developments.[1] In Berlin, he received a cable from Nanking inviting him to become minister of education in the provisional government being formed in that city.[2] We can imagine his excitement on being asked to assume such a significant position. In Germany, he had become an admirer of the famous nineteenth-century educator Wilhelm von Humboldt, founder of the University of Berlin and visionary of the university as a haven for research and scholastic freedom, as well as a center for a national and cultural revival. As an anarchist, Ts'ai was morally pledged to avoid political entanglements, but the temptation was too great. As minister of education, Ts'ai may have hoped to preside over a rebirth of China.

In 1912, Ts'ai returned to China and was sworn in with the rest of the provisional cabinet. In March, when the coalition government composed of representatives from Nanking and supporters of Yüan Shih-k'ai in Peking was formed, Ts'ai was a member of the Kuomintang in the ten-man cabinet, despite his growing suspicion of Yüan's motives. He immediately planned to transform the educational system into an instrument which would reflect new republican ideals.

Education under the Empire. The educational structure that Ts'ai inherited in 1912 differed greatly from the system under which he had been educated as a youth. China's defeats by foreign powers at the end of the nineteenth century had convinced many that a reform of China's educational system was a matter of priority. As the new century dawned, the elderly statesman Chang Chih-tung was planning a program of educational reform in an effort to save the old dynasty. The educational system he was attempting to change was barely affected by Western ideas and technology. A few schools had been opened along the coast to train Chinese personnel in specialized fields such as interpreting and naval science, but the system as a whole did not reflect such innovations. There was no system of national public education. Earning an assignment in the governmental bureaucracy was still the accepted aim of education. And training in China's privately supported schools emphasized knowledge of the classics, rather than the modern social and natural sciences. Finally, there was the civil-service examination system, the fearsome entranceway for ambitious students to a career in the civil service.

For some time, progressive intellectuals had been aware of the relationship between the old educational system and China's inability to reform, but their efforts had been stubbornly resisted by conservatives, convinced that if the Confucian-oriented educational system was abandoned, the moral disintegration of Chinese society would set in. Chang Chih-tung, a Confucianist but an advocate of moderate reform, was prepared to undertake an operation—to reform the educational system to meet the changing needs of Chinese society, while preserving the "national essence," the study of the Confucian classics which, he firmly believed, must remain the basis for molding the moral character of the student.

Chang's reforms, achieved over a period of years with little resistance from the empress dowager in Peking, stressed reforms in several areas: the creation of a national system of public education, beginning with schools at the elementary level and culminating in nationally run universities in the large cities, replacing or incorporating the privately owned schools of the traditional period; the creation of a Ministry of Education to provide centralized direction for the entire system; the elimination of the civil-service examination as a testing mechanism for entrance into the bureaucracy, and the inclusion of examinations for government careers within the school system itself; broadening the curriculum to include courses in the sciences and foreign languages; and the elimination of the eight-legged essay as the basis for literary style. Chang also recommended study abroad programs to assimilate foreign knowledge, so necessary to the survival of China; the development of a separate system of schools to provide education for the first time to girls; a broadened concept of the aims of education, in order to provide for the general enlightenment of the Chinese population and not simply turn out candidates for the civil-service examination. As a

43

reminder that the new system was still loyal to Confucius, study of the classics was maintained as the heart of the curriculum.[3]

Chang had gone as far as possible on the *t'i-yung* philosophy. He had opened the door to new knowledge while protecting the classical heart of the educational system from the effects of cultural erosion. In 1906, responding to the criticisms of Liang Ch'i-ch'ao, the new Ministry of Education clarified the aims of the new system—loyalty to the emperor; respect for Confucius; training in public morality, the military spirit, and utilitarianism. In its aims and structure, the new system was patterned after education in Germany and Japan. It was definitely a step into the future, for Chinese education was becoming broader in scope. Although no concrete steps had been taken to develop a system of universal education, the matter had been discussed. No doubt, the new system had an immediate effect on China. The new attitudes of Chinese students in the modern schools of Shanghai reflected this change. Although many of the Shanghai schools bursting with revolutionary sentiment were privately run, they probably reflected the broad changes taking place in public schools as well. To progressives, the change was welcome. China's youth was increasingly exposed to Western knowledge, to Darwinism, to democracy, to Marx and Russian nihilism. The conservatives, on the other hand, were disturbed because students were unruly, sloppy in dress, and arbitrary in cutting and dropping classes. For good or ill, Chinese education was being Westernized.[4]

Proposals for a New System of Education. In these circumstances, Ts'ai Yüan-p'ei returned to take charge of China's educational system. He wasted little time in laying his new philosophy of reform before the Chinese public. In the spring of 1912, he published an article in the journal *Eastern Miscellany* [Tung-fang tsa-chih], setting forth the philosophy which would underlie his educational reform proposals. His basic theme was a plea for mutual assistance and gradualism, for a belief in the ultimate powers of evolution and the oneness of humanity. Ts'ai feared that rising nationalism might cut the bloom off the humanist rose, and he hoped to instill a faith in humanity that would carry China to a cultural renaissance. Mankind, he said, is like two men in a boat: if they don't share the rowing, how will they ever reach the shore?[5]

He had also returned to China with ideas concerning a new philosophy of education, and shortly after his arrival he presented some basic concepts to the educated public. The February 1912 issue of *Chiao-yü tsa-chih* [Educational Review] contained his now-famous article "My Views on the Aims of Education" [Tui-yü chiao-yü fang-chen chih i-chien] in which he spelled out his proposals for the restructuring of education in China.[6] Ts'ai made clear that one of China's greatest needs was a new philosophy of education. As he explained it, the goals of education under the empire had been essentially political: to inculcate in the student respect for authority, loyalty to the dynasty, and obedience to the principles of Confucius. In such a system, however, the needs of the individual were subordinated to the requirements of the government and the ruling oligarchy. In a republic, on the other hand, education should serve the needs of the individual and of society as a whole. It should service not only political requirements, but also the happiness of the private citizen.

Such ideas contrasted not only with the traditional system, but with the views of prominent members of the new government as well, who saw education as an instrument for serving the immediate political aims of the state. Ts'ai, therefore, needed to devise a system which would assuage the potential resistance by his colleagues and further the realization of his goals. He divided his program into two parts, one to serve the political aim of strengthening society, and the other to transcend politics and educate China's youth in an understanding of internationalism.

Ts'ai saw three ways in which education might be subordinated to national requirements—national military education, utilitarian education, and ethical education. In the present state of the world, he admitted, education must contribute to the preservation and development of the state. Not generally sympathetic to military interests, Ts'ai admitted that there were valid reasons for keeping military education in republican China, not only for national defense, but to prevent the military establishment from becoming a separate and powerful class.

The second determinant of national strength was the level of resources and human talent. Utilitarian education would attempt to raise the material and technological level of the nation in order to further national prosperity. Ts'ai, believing that material and spiritual progress were compatible, had no objection to including this aspect in his program. The third quality, ethical education, would attempt to provide a moral basis for society, inculcating in every citizen the moral standards necessary to prevent internal oppression and exploitation, as well as obedience to the law. Here, however, Ts'ai rejected the traditional ethical basis of Chinese society, the Confucian five relationships (enjoining loyalty and obedience by minister to king, son to father, younger to older brother, wife to husband, and friend to friend), and suggested that republican ethics should be based on the French revolutionary concept of liberty, equality, and fraternity. To illustrate his point, he equated liberty with the Chinese concept of righteousness [*i*]. Righteousness is what Confucius meant when he said that a good man could not be corrupted by wealth and power [*fu kuei pu neng kuo, wei wu pu neng chü*]. Equality is the equivalent of the traditional Chinese concept of *shu* ("reciprocity") and corresponds to the Confucian phrase

"Do not do unto others what you would not have them do unto you" [*chi so pu yü wu shih yü jen*]. Without a policy which will guarantee equality, Ts'ai asserted, the Chinese people will demand equal treatment and not receive it, and what we know as freedom and equality will be impossible to achieve. Fraternity, he concluded, is like the Confucian concept of benevolence [*jen*]. As the Master said: "Do unto others as you would have them do unto you" [*chi yü li erh li jen, chi yü ta erh ta jen*].

The above three points were concerned with improving the material conditions in Chinese society. They were designed to placate members of the new government who were more concerned with national survival than with utopian visions. By themselves, Ts'ai's reforms were hardly innovative: except for the replacement of the five relationships with the French revolutionary slogan, they reflected the reforms in education that took place during the old dynasty. The heart of Ts'ai's program concerned transcendental education which would, no doubt, arouse controversy. Education, he asserted in his article, must be directed at more than achieving "the greatest material happiness for the greatest number." Man requires the satisfaction of spiritual as well as material needs. Education, therefore, must have a broader aim, to help humanity understand the real world beyond the phenomenal world. Ts'ai's program for transcendental education comprised two aspects, world-outlook education and aesthetics education. World-outlook education would acquaint students with the religions, philosophies, and cultures of all human societies in order to demonstrate the essential unity of all mankind, thus reducing the localism and superstition which characterize the Chinese. Aesthetics education would help to eliminate greed and prejudice from the material world. For these final aspects of his new program, emphasis was placed on the need to encourage the individual to develop his own talent and to achieve greater spiritual happiness.

Ts'ai had been exposed to several educational theories while abroad, to the French system of decentralized schools, to Pestalozzi's teaching methods, to Dewey's democratic education, and he had other proposals related to the reform of Chinese education: he was prepared to accept the Japanese three-stage–four-level system as appropriate to China's needs. He was anxious, however, to realize substantial decentralization, with basic decision-making apparatus at the district level, and a loose direction from the central Ministry of Education.[7] Ts'ai also intended to establish universities in all provinces and to place administrative control of all schools within each province under the direction of university authorities. Peking University would naturally become China's greatest institute of learning, but he hoped that others could be formed, notably in Nanking, Hankow, Chengtu, and Canton. It was Ts'ai's theory that it was necessary to begin at the university rather than the elementary level. This seems to contradict his emphasis on the establishment of a system of mass education. But Ts'ai simply looked at the problem from the standpoint of teachers, not students. The basic obstacle, of course, was the lack of trained teachers, a problem which could only be overcome by an expansion at the university level. Ts'ai once commented that the stimulation for the national and cultural revival of nineteenth-century Germany had come from her dedicated elementary school teachers.[8] Once a number of teachers were trained, obligatory education could be established. For adults without any exposure to education, he proposed the establishment of a social education office which would extend knowledge to the masses by means of libraries, newspapers, lecture halls, and language reform. To bring women into the system, he proposed the expansion of female education in China, including the establishment of coeducational schools at the elementary level. Finally, he proposed the elimination of classics education in elementary and middle schools, and the development of textbooks to reflect the new republican ideals.[9]

To a degree, Ts'ai's proposals were not a significant departure from the existing educational system—the emphasis on public morality, military training, and utilitarian education had been recognized and initiated by Chang Chih-tung. The trend toward obligatory education and female education had already begun in the late dynastic period; even in his emphasis on aesthetics, he was reflecting the traditional Confucian belief that art and music could help mold the human personality. There was a revolutionary side to his proposals, however. In his emphasis on internationalism, decentralization, and the individual needs of the student, Ts'ai was running counter to established practice. Decentralization and the emphasis on individual freedom would therefore limit the power of the state to use education for its own aims. By emphasizing world-outlook education, he would weaken national sentiment. Many republicans would agree with monarchists in opposing these aspects of Ts'ai's program.

When Ts'ai took over the ministry in January 1912, he issued temporary orders designed to incorporate opening steps in the comprehensive reform program he planned for China. Education in the classics was forbidden at the elementary school level and would be replaced by courses in handicrafts and drawing. Teaching of Confucian ethics was to be given in readers, not in the original classical version. Elementary education was to become coeducational, and texts at all levels were to be "republicanized." His program would be a heady draft for the new Republic to swallow, and in July 1912, to obtain sufficient support he convened an Emergency Central Educational Conference of educators from all sections of the country. As he opened the conference, Ts'ai explained his program and urged Chinese educators not to be afraid to strike out on a new path. He placed particular emphasis on the need to use education to unify the nation, to decentralize the school system, and to ensure that the minority races received equal treatment, and finally to move toward the establishment of a unified written language for China.[10]

His speech emphasized that education under a republic should attempt to develop the specific abilities of individual students, and not merely satisfy the wishes of the government. Once again he stressed the need to complement military and utilitarian education with the transcendental education he had earlier outlined. Finally, he cautioned his audience not to vacillate between periods of self-love [*tzu-ta*] and self-hate [*tzu-ch'i*]. Self-love arises when China overestimates the values of her "four thousand years of culture." Then, after China loses a few battles, her self-confidence diminishes and lapses into blind imitation of others.

The conference was receptive to many of Ts'ai's ideas, but there was considerable resistance to many basic aspects of his program. The structural and curricular reforms were adopted with minor changes, and the provisions concerning coeducational schools and the establishment of an office of social education were also accepted. In line with his desires, education in the classics was eliminated in all lower and middle-level schools.[11]

Despite his attempt to pad new concepts with familiar ones, Ts'ai's basic idea of promoting internationalism and stressing individual development clashed with the opinions of many at the conference who viewed education more as an instrument to mobilize the population for social goals determined by the state than as a means of developing individual character. Consequently, the government program which was eventually adopted reflected a distinct dilution of his original proposals. The three elements of military, utilitarian, and ethical education were included in the new statement of educational aims, but his new morality was rejected in favor of the traditional five relationships. As for the transcendental aspects of his program, the part relating to aesthetics education was included, but world-outlook education was entirely left out.[12]

Dissatisfied with President Yüan Shih-k'ai's domineering behavior, Ts'ai resigned his position before the conference had adjourned.[13] Perhaps he should not have been so discouraged, for the changes he had helped to fashion during his brief tenure as minister were to result in major changes in China's educational system. The early years of the Republic witnessed an expansion in the number of schools, tripling over the four-year period, and a quadrupling of the number of students. The social education program managed to establish a number of public lecture halls at the district level throughout the country. Chinese schools increasingly exposed young students to Western ideas and new attitudes: after 1912, emphasis in the textbooks was placed on patriotism, progress through the development of science and technology, internationalism as an ultimate goal, the need to eliminate harmful customs such as disorderliness and lack of public spirit, and emulation of the progressive attitudes of the West.[14] By 1916, the new school system was becoming the focus of rising idealism for the future and growing discontent with the present.

If progressives felt that the changes instituted in 1912 could be seen as a qualified success, for President Yüan Shih-k'ai and his fellow conservatives the consequences of educational reform gave cause for profound disquiet. The new freedom in Chinese schools had not only opened the doors to modern knowledge, but (in Yüan's eyes) to moral disintegration as well. By 1913, he was complaining of student misbehavior and widespread transgression of school regulations. Conservatives began to call for a return to law and order in the schools. Blaming the trouble on the lack of student exposure to Confucian ethics, they agitated for a resumption of training in the classics. In early 1915, the government decreed a number of changes in the educational system by which courses in the classics were resumed at lower and middle level, and a new set of educational aims was issued, stressing not only patriotism but respect for Confucius and Mencius, self-control, and prevention of selfish struggle.[15] However, in October 1916, shortly after his death, Yüan's revisions were dropped.

In 1912, there were other problems more serious for the Republic than a new educational system, at least from the short-range point of view. Many of these problems were related to the fact that the center of power in China was in Peking where Yüan Shih-k'ai ruled, surrounded by a coterie of military and civilian advisers. Yüan, unlike Sun Yat-sen, had no strong ideological bent toward the establishment of a Republic on the Western model, and a conflict soon arose between supporters of Yüan and the Kuomintang even before the formation of a coalition government in March 1912.

This first issue concerned the location of the new capital of China. Sun Yat-sen desired to locate it at Nanking in central China. Realizing that his own power was based in Peking, Yüan did not wish to have the center of power shifted to the Yangtse Valley.[16] On 29 February 1912, Sun, now provisional president in Nanking, sent Ts'ai and two others to Peking where they invited Yüan to be installed as president of the Republic in Nanking. Although Sun suspected that Yüan would be unwilling to leave Peking, he decided to try to bring him to Nanking.[17] On the night of their arrival, the delegates were treated to a mutiny of military units around Peking, protesting, among other things, the pending departure of Yüan for Nanking. Whether Yüan had staged the mutiny himself is a matter of dispute. Ts'ai and his colleagues felt that the compromise might easily be shattered by this minor matter, and after some harassment by the restless soldiery, he cabled Sun on 2 March, advising him to accept Peking as the capital. Nanking reluctantly accepted his suggestion on 7 March, and Yüan was installed at Peking. As a result of this incident, however, Ts'ai was unhappy that the spiritual unity of the new leadership had been shattered. Eventually, he publicly declared his disapproval of Yüan's attitude, stating that the unity of the nation was more important than individual convenience, and that the individual should sacrifice such personal convenience for the sake of society.[18]

After this initial agreement, T'ang Shao-yi formed a government including Ts'ai as minister of education and three other Kuomintang members in the ten-man cabinet. Ts'ai hesitated to serve under Yüan, but it is alleged that when he heard Sun was angry with him for failing to persuade Yüan to come to Nanking, Ts'ai decided to accept the position.[19] In any case, a new disagreement arose over the form of government, and Ts'ai again found himself at loggerheads with Yüan's faction. The Kuomintang members of the cabinet wanted the new republican system to be modeled after the cabinet systems in Europe, with the executive responsible in major matters to the legislative branch. Yüan, on the other hand, favored a presidential system which placed little limitation on his authority and allowed him to decide major matters without referring to the legislative body. Ts'ai himself supported the cabinet system, but was unable to stem the growing tide of Yüan's power.

Ts'ai's opposition to the presidential system reflected his distrust not only of Yüan, but of overweening governmental authority in any form, stemming partly from his exposure to anarchism. He felt that centralized government was encouraged by the evil elements in society. The president, in his view, "does not need to have ability. . . . Only virtue is required. If the president has no real power, then the position of Head of State is only an honorary position, not much different from the award of an order of merit. In such a case, who would take great pains to obtain such empty glory?" Under these circumstances, "the presidency will not be the prey of strong and ambitious competitors, and our national character can be purged of its character of subservience."[20]

It became apparent, however, that Yüan had no intention of referring major matters to the legislature. When premier T'ang Shao-yi felt that he too was being ignored by the president, T'ang and the four Kuomintang members resigned together in July 1912. Yüan appointed the vice-minister of education, Fan Yüan-lien, to replace Ts'ai in office. Officials at the ministry suggested that Ts'ai be appointed to the chancellorship at Peking University, but Yüan refused in indignant tones:

> Mr. Ts'ai is a member of the Kuomintang and is a fervent advocate of revolution, and many of the incidents occurring

these days are connected with him; if I make him chancellor of Peking University, and assist him in cultivating revolutionary talent, the government will soon be in a hopeless situation and my own position will not be secure.[21]

Yüan, obviously, did not underrate ˎTs'ai's persuasive abilities. Actually, the distrust was mutual. Ts'ai's early suspicion of Yüan, evident in his letters from Berlin to Wu Chih-hui, had, in his eyes, been justified by events. Even on Yüan's death in 1916, he could not hide his dislike:

Mr. Yüan was not only much more evil than the average man in society, he represented in himself the three evils of the old society—bureaucracy [kuan-liao], pedantry [hsüeh-chiu], and necromancy [fang-shih]. He feared the strong and oppressed the weak, cheated the public and favored the greedy, talked with honey in his mouth but carried a sword for your belly, and indulged all of his luxurious desires. He was the personification of official ignorance, worship of the emperor, in the Temple of Heaven, and the advocation of the study of the classics in elementary schools. . . . This was his use of all the traditional pedantry. He used all the old mystical humbug of the old society— oaths in the Temple of the God of War, praying in church, flattering and greasing his ministers, and relying on necromancers to cure disease. With Mr. Yüan removed, is it not possible that these social poisons will disappear as well?[22]

Fortunately, Ts'ai was able to escape Yüan and return to Germany to study on funds from the ministry. He was evidently disgusted with the Kuomintang and with the political situation in general, charging in late 1912 that the old T'ung-meng-hui was disintegrating.[23] Ts'ai remained in Leipzig for one year where he studied cultural history. In the summer of 1913, he received a telegram from China asking him to mediate in a new dispute between the Yüan faction and the Kuomintang. Kuomintang leader Sung Chiao-jen had been assassinated by Yüan's henchmen in March, and members of the Kuomintang had attempted to drive Yüan out of power by military force. Ts'ai counseled against the use of force to settle the conflict, while simultaneously attempting to persuade Yüan to resign. His advice had no effect, however, and the rebels were defeated.[24] That fall, Ts'ai settled in Paris until the war broke out and then moved to southern France.

In some respects, this period was the least productive of his mature life. With Yüan in power, Ts'ai was temporarily at loose ends. Much of his time was spent in writing and research. He wrote a primer on philosophy entitled Introduction to Philosophy [Che-hsueh ta-kang], based on the thoughts of Richter, Paulsen, and Wundt. He also wrote an analysis of his favorite classical novel *Dream of the Red Chamber*. He also attempted to translate Kant's studies on aesthetics and write a history of European art, although neither work was finished.[25] Clearly, Ts'ai was marking time until the situation improved.

5

The Rising Tide

In the winter of 1916, Ts'ai Yüan-p'ei received an invitation from Fan Yüan-lien, his successor at the Ministry of Education, to become chancellor of Peking University. President Yüan Shih-k'ai had died earlier in the year, and the climate had improved for Ts'ai's return to China.

Ts'ai's position at Peita (the diminutive form for Peking University) would, no doubt, enable him to influence the affairs of the nation. Peking University was the first modern university in China. It had made little progress, however, under a succession of undistinguished chancellors in meeting requirements for a modern center of higher education. In 1916, when he was invited to become head of the institution, it had earned an unenviable reputation. Generally indifferent to scholarship, students concentrated their efforts on receiving diplomas, the necessary step to becoming government officials. Instructors, affected by the students' indifference to scholarship, developed a lackadaisical attitude toward teaching duties. Unfortunately, students devoted more time to drinking and gambling than to their studies.[1]

When Ts'ai arrived in Shanghai from France, some of his friends advised him to reject the offer of the chancellorship because the corruption at the university was endemic and could only harm his reputation. Others argued that the situation was not hopeless and that Ts'ai should take the job. Opinion in the ranks of the Kuomintang was also divided, some opposing any cooperation with the Peking warlord regime, but Sun Yat-sen himself approved of the offer.[2] Fortunately for the university, Ts'ai agreed with Sun's diagnosis and decided to accept the appointment. The basic problem at the institution, he decided, was the debilitating influence of the examination system. Although it had been abolished by the old dynasty in 1906, its influence lingered on, and students felt that the system was simply a stepladder to a government career.

Ts'ai's early years as chancellor were destined to be the height of his public career. On assuming his position in January 1917, Ts'ai immediately made it clear that the university would play a new role in the affairs of the nation. In his opening speech as chancellor, he expressed some of his views regarding the future of the institution.[3] No longer would the university act as a haven for aspirants to government careers; in the future it would be primarily an institution devoted to study and research, and its second effort would be the improvement of the moral tone of the nation. Ts'ai obviously had nineteenth-century Germany in his mind's eye. In a letter to his anarchist colleague Wang Ching-wei, asking him to teach Chinese literature at the university, Ts'ai made the following historical comparison: It was the German philosopher Fichte, he said, whose patriotic speeches saved Prussia from disintegration before the Napoleonic onslaught and sparked the German cultural revival. Wang could become a Chinese Fichte, reviving the spirit of Chinese youth through the *"real* national heritage."[4]

Ts'ai was confident that internal reorganization and a stress on scholarship would sweep out much of the apathy and corruption within the university.[5] Therefore, his primary aim was the development of a more democratic administrative structure and a new interest in scholarship. He gradually streamlined the administration to permit greater participation in university decisions by the faculty, and greater self-regulation for the students. A legislative body of deans was organized to help direct the institution. A faculty assembly was also established to recommend curriculum changes. The revised curriculum stressed the dual nature of Arts and Sciences and encouraged a spirit of learning and research. To build an interest in scholarship, Ts'ai set up research institutes in the natural and social sciences, broadened the language and modern literature offerings, and organized speaking clubs in which music, art, journalism, and political science were discussed.[6]

Ts'ai's ambitions for Peking University were not limited, however, to organizational reform. He wanted to transform the university into an institution designed to create the intellectual leadership for China. Convinced that the masses had to be committed to the idea of reform before true modernization could take place, he hoped that Peita would become a great institute of learning and the training ground of an educated elite which would spread knowledge throughout the nation. Ts'ai's basic aim was to provide an educational system which would encourage the fullest development of the individual character and talent in all students, thereby producing a number of Chinese scholars renowned in all fields of endeavor. He was convinced that a nation's reputation was built more on the strength of its intellectual and cultural attainments than on its military prowess or political influence. Such intellectual excellence could be attained only in an atmosphere favoring the search for truth and knowledge. Consequently, he encouraged freedom of opinion and invited scholars of various beliefs to teach at the university. Any idea which could be rationally held and had not been eliminated by natural selection was allowed to be expressed. With that in mind, Ts'ai attempted to employ faculty representatives of a wide variety of conflicting views. Ch'en Tu-hsiu, editor of the radical journal *New Youth* and, in later years, a founder of the Communist party, became dean of the College of Literature.[7] As members of the faculty, Hu Shih and Ch'ien Hsüan-t'ung, supporters of the vernacular movements, subjected the Chinese classical tradition to rigorous analysis. Others new members, such as Ts'ai's ex-anarchist colleague Liu Shih-p'ei and Huang Chi-kang, were conservative in their political tendencies and defenders of the traditional literary style. In early republican China, where the younger generation was passionately devoted to the discussion of new ideas, the university became a forum of cultural and intellectual interchange.[8]

Under Ts'ai's direction, Peking University had thus become an instrument of feverish intellectual activity in the young Republic. Ts'ai's provocative style had stimulated the rise of a new political and intellectual consciousness among the students at the university and at neighboring educational institutions. Soft-spoken, affable, and accessible, he symbolized receptivity to youth and to the new knowledge pouring in from the West. And in his personal demeanor, he epitomized the best qualities of the traditional Confucian gentleman [*chün tzu*]. A defender of the dignity of man, catholic in his outlook, synthesizing East and West, Ts'ai was the quintessence of the renaissance spirit pervading the young Republic. Under his direction, the university had become the center of the progressive movement and the vanguard of change in the new China.

The Spirit of the New Culture Movement. Beyond the challenges of Peking University lay broader questions of social change momentous to the future of China. Ts'ai's appointment to Peita coincided with the rise of a movement among progressive intellectuals to initiate changes in China's institutions and values—the famous New Culture Movement. The disappointment generated by the aftermath of the 1911 revolution caused the formation of the new movement. The accession of Yüan Shih-k'ai to the presidency in 1912 had temporarily dammed up the emotions of the immediate prerevolutionary period. His character and alleged monarchical ambitions inspired little confidence among reform-minded Chinese. Where it had been hoped that the new Republic would once again play a leading role in the affairs of Asia, Yüan's government was under growing pressure from abroad, culminating in Japan's Twenty-One Demands of 1915. Where progressives had seen the 1911 revolution as the opening wedge for a "transvaluation of values," a reform which would eliminate the dead hand of Confucian tradition and bring Chinese institutions in line with modern needs, President Yüan's response was a know-nothing authoritarianism and reliance on Confucian ethics. By 1915, there was even talk of restoring the dynastic system. Angered by Yüan's dictatorial policies and frustrated over the failure of 1911 to spark social change, members of the intellectual community prepared to renew the struggle for a new China.

It is difficult to summarize the ideals that motivated the progressive movement during the years of the early Republic. The New Culture Movement was almost too diverse to support meaningful generalizations. It was characterized by contradictory impulses—idealistic humanitarianism contrasted with rabid nationalism, utopian egalitarianism clashed with overt acceptance of the need for an elitist leadership, and despair over the present combined with hope for the future. And there was a faddish quality about much of the intellectual ferment during the period. New ideas from the West were introduced with little thought or analysis. Theories were adopted and abandoned with amazing suddenness. Discoveries of new schools of thought could cause young intellectuals to change their philosophical beliefs in days. As Chiang Monlin once complained, ideas were coming in so fast that intellectuals simply could not absorb them all.

The essential causes for the movement are no mystery. With the failure of 1911, Chinese intellectuals were searching for a formula that would awaken China and begin a process of rapid social and cultural rejuvenation. The spirit of the new movement was symbolized by the phrase "Down with the old, up with the new." Almost all aspects of the traditional order—the literary language, the family system, state Confucianism, and the subordination of the female—were attacked, and considered harmful to the new China.

Confucianism had been the object of progressive attacks for years. What distinguished the Culturalites from their predecessors, however, was the vehemence of their attack on the old order. The elder generation of K'ang Yu-wei and Liang Ch'i-ch'ao, and even revolutionaries such as Sun Yat-sen, had distinguished between the *dregs* of traditional society and those elements of the Confucian-Mencian humanist heritage which should be preserved in China. For the new generation, there was little in the old order that was worth saving. Wu Yü, perhaps the most vicious of the anti-Confucianists, summed up the attitude of a generation in the progressive journal *New Youth* when he described Confucianism as a morality which had a debilitating effect on the human spirit. Less savage was the writer Lu Hsün, whose short stories in the same journal excoriated the virtues of Confucian civilization as nothing better than a wen on a man's face.

The new generation greatly admired modern Western culture. There was an avid interest in everything Western—radical journals published stories and articles about Tolstoi, Ibsen, and Shaw and detailed analyses of the legal systems and political institutions of Western democracy; educators published the latest information about educational trends in Western Europe and the United States; new literary and philosophical currents were discussed and imitated. Few showed any sense of balance or discrimination, for it was not a time for objectivity. Although Hu Shih, who had just returned from study in the United States as a disciple of John Dewey, expressed a need for a critical analysis of tradition and the retention of the good from the past, and although Li Ta-chao wanted to synthesize the *activism* of the West with the *spiritual* qualities of China, the overall spirit of the time was one of Westernization.[9]

In essence, the Culturalites had reacted to the failure of political revolution by turning to cultural issues, to the reform of society from the ground up. The rise of Yüan Shih-k'ai had demonstrated that a simple grafting of Western political institutions onto the lifeless body of Confucian society was inadequate. Liang Ch'i-ch'ao had talked of the "new man" a decade before, but Liang had since become a man of gradualism and compromise with the old society. For the Culturalites, the future was now.

Ts'ai Yüan-p'ei and Democracy. The appointment of Ts'ai Yüan-p'ei to the leadership of Peking University seemed providential. If the New Culture Movement based its program on the liberal humanism of Western Europe and the United States, this, too, was the wellspring from which flowed much of Ts'ai's philosophy. Ts'ai soon became a leader in the new thought tide and welcomed the introduction of ideas from abroad, as well as the attacks on the old order.

For Ts'ai, one of the primary keys to building a modern China lay in mastering the concept of democracy. Western democratic institutions had fascinated Chinese intellectuals for over a generation, and by the early Republic had built a strong base of support in the progressive community. Although there was a feverish interest in democracy, and progressive journals contained articles which praised the democratic heritage of the West, the unifying and "state-strengthening" qualities of democracy had truly appealed to many Chinese, more than its capacity to promote individual freedom.

This issue has been discussed by Jerome Grieder in his recent study *Hu Shih and the Chinese Renaissance.* Not until Hu and the rise of the New Culture Movement, he states, did the progressives in China begin to see the distinction between public and private spheres in a Western democratic system, and the importance in a democracy of maximizing the individual's rights.[10] In defending individualism, Hu did not mean to deny that community needs imposed limitations on individual freedom, and from Dewey he drew the distinction between a selfish ego-centered individualism [*wei-wu chu-i*] and a responsible sense of individuality within the larger community [*ko-hsing chu-i*].[11] For the

Chinese Deweyites, individualism could not exist outside of a community, and the individual and society had to be of equal importance. Unlike their predecessors, however, they emphasized individual rights and the concept of voluntarism.

For a time, this emphasis on the individualistic character of Western democracy made a deep impression on new culture intellectuals. The articles written on democracy during this period indicate that stress was on the necessity to make democracy a living concept in China, by making it an active part of school, home, and society. Democracy was seen as a way of life, and not just a matter of governmental institutions. The belief that democracy, in Grieder's words, is less a matter of specific institutions than a state of mind, was a common symptom of the period.[12] In this sense, the new progressives had grasped a point that had escaped earlier generations.

Ts'ai's emotional commitment to the democratic ideal was as strong or stronger than most of his contemporaries. In 1912, he had attempted to inculcate democratic principles in society through the educational system. Then, when he became chancellor of Peita, he initiated a number of changes designed to create a more democratic system of self-government. In several speeches and articles, he discussed the problem of achieving individual freedom within human society. In the conflict between the individual and state, Ts'ai placed himself on the side of the individual in the preservation of human rights, often noting the Mencian tradition in which the people are of value and the monarch is of secondary importance. This attitude is evident in his approach to education, where he stressed the need for a system which would maximize the opportunity for individual development of character and minimize the interference of state authority. This emphasis on civil liberty often involved him in the active defense of individuals who had been deprived of their civil rights by oppressive governments.[13]

Ts'ai's belief in individual freedom was supplemented by an emotional commitment to the progress of society as a whole, and the moral obligation of the individual to place the community's needs above his own. Individual freedom, in his eyes, was tied to a higher duty—the voluntary obligation to serve the needs of society.[14] This, of course, is the dilemma of a democratic society, and many of Ts'ai's predecessors had faced it by accepting the need for coercion. Ts'ai hoped that the reconciliation between individual and social interests could be achieved by moral suasion, and his articles and speeches during the new culture period were filled with exhortations to virtue and self-improvement.[15]

Ts'ai's concept of man's role in society was an amalgam of modern Western individualism and the humanist side of Confucian ethics. Prepared to preach the necessity of subordinating private interests to the community, he was determined to abjure the use of legal sanctions to obtain compliance. In the perspective of Chinese thought, he had continued the dualism of self-cultivation and service to society in Confucianism and come down strongly on the humanist side of the traditional argument. In the context of the New Culture Movement, he showed a clear resemblance to Hu Shih, although Ts'ai probably put greater emphasis on the need for community service than did his younger contemporary.

Critics could charge that Ts'ai had ignored the dilemma of individual and society by assuming that men could perceive the existence of a natural "harmony of interests" between individual rights and community needs. Moreover, critics could say that Ts'ai's voluntarism had little meaning in a China where the masses were ignorant and superstitious and where the warlords were not interested in drawing the fine distinctions sketched by the intellectuals.

Science and the New China. Western science was seen by most Culturalites as a wonder weapon, capable of solving the problems of human livelihood and serving as the instrument for material progress. Some saw it as a virtual replacement for religion. Ts'ai had faith in science and often had observed that China's historical weakness lay in her failure to develop science as rapidly as the West. He was unusual, however, in sensing the potential danger from an over-reliance on the powers of modern technology. In 1916, when K'ang Yu-wei advocated the institution of Confucianism as a state religion, Ts'ai voiced his firm opposition to the project.[16] Although he opposed the idea of a state religion, he felt that man had a spiritual sense that could not be satisfied by philosophical materialism. Occasionally, he indicated that if China were to rely solely on science for development, she would become rich and powerful, but would lack the high-mindedness necessary to reach the final *Ta-t'ung.*[17]

Ts'ai's answer was in aesthetics. Through his study in Leipzig, he came to feel the effects of the environment on human behavior and recommended that aesthetic education be started even before the birth of the child. Prenatal homes, designed in Renaissance or Greek style, should be provided for pregnant women. Nature should be nearby so that prospective mothers would have the opportunity to relax and avoid tension. After the child is born, he should be exposed to art and music in his early years, and when he begins to attend primary school, he should receive formal artistic training.[18]

Ts'ai realized that the Chinese government could not be persuaded to adopt aesthetics education solely because of its contribution to distant goals. From the bureaucratic point of view, religion provided cohesion to the state and support for its goals—a fact K'ang Yu-wei had not neglected in his defense of Confucianism. If aesthetics was to be given serious attention by the advocates of militant nationalism and self-strengthening, Ts'ai would have to demonstrate its usefulness in providing an integrative force for the nation. In a speech given in December 1919, he attempted to do that, claiming that European greatness was not a product of Christianity or of science alone, but of science and art.[19]

Ts'ai's advocacy of aesthetics as a vital element in the reconstruction of China was briefly successful in academic circles. In general, however, his theory was greeted with a mixture of condescension and indifference, and made little imprint on Chinese society. Nevertheless, Ts'ai was undaunted and continued to press for a greater role for aesthetics until the end of his life.

Education and Moral Transformation. The generation of intellectuals who matured in the early Republic believed that the major key to a modern, democratic society was the creation of a new man. The preoccupation with education as a major factor in social reform was a quality that ran through the entire progressive movement, characteristic of moderates as well as the propagandists of revolution. If anything, this belief was increased as a result of the 1911 revolution, which showed that institutional reform, by itself, did not necessarily lead to the realization of a democratic society.

While this trend lasted, it coincided in great measure with Ts'ai's ideas. In his eyes, too, the key lay in education. "If we want to achieve all [our] cultural goals," he said, "they must be understood by the majority of the populace. So we must begin by universalizing education." Because of Ts'ai's educational reforms suggested in 1912, education was moving in the direction desired by the progressives. Chinese students were now being exposed to a different set of values. Textbooks put into use in the postrevolutionary period not only emphasized patriotism and national consciousness, but praised Western civilization, internationalism, and the doctrine of progress.[20]

There was still a long way to go. Only a small percentage of Chinese children were in school. At the university level, remnants of the old examination system perpetuated traditional attitudes. The logjam on the modernization of the educational system began to break in 1918. The number of Western-trained educators increased during the early republican years, and educational conferences, led by reform-minded educators such as Ts'ai, Chiang Monlin, Fan Yüan-lien, Ho Ping-sung, and T'ao Meng-ho, demanded a further remodeling of the educational system. Ts'ai urged greater attention to educational techniques being developed in the West.[21] The American educator-philosopher John Dewey was the strongest influence on Ts'ai and other educators. Ts'ai had been an admirer of Dewey for several years, and his thinking on education during the new culture period reflected Dewey's ideas.

Spurred by the visit of Dewey to China from 1919 to 1921, educational reform became a major issue during the first decade of the new Republic. Ts'ai utilized numerous educational conferences to make the following proposals for the reform of the educational system: education should aim to cultivate a wholesome personality and develop a republican spirit; military training in schools should be eliminated and replaced by physical drill; the courses on personal ethics [*hsiu-shen-k'o*] should be replaced by courses on civic training.[22] Some of these proposals were accepted by the Ministry of Education. They were not formally proclaimed, however, and in many cases did not take effect until the educational reform of 1922.

National Unification and Language Reform. Of primary concern to educational reformers was the problem of language reform which, in China, was of direct relevance to the elimination of mass illiteracy. There were, however, several facets to the question of reform: the unification of the spoken tongue, simplification of the written language to facilitate learning, and the replacement of literary Chinese by the vernacular as the primary medium for literary expression. Ts'ai was to become involved at many points in the language controversy.

The movement to create a national language understood by all Chinese had begun in the first decade of the twentieth century, as government and radicals saw it as a tool in national unification. After 1903, the government began to push Mandarin as the language of instruction in Chinese schools. Ts'ai himself had become interested in the relevance of language reform to cultural change. In Shanghai, he had used the vernacular as an instrument in propagandizing for the revolutionary cause. While in Europe, he became acquainted with Esperanto, the most ambitious attempt to create an international language transcending national and cultural boundaries. Ts'ai believed that Esperanto, an international means of communication, would limit prejudice and forward progress to the final *Ta-t'ung*. In 1912, as minister of education, he convened a conference of language experts to discuss Wu Chih-hui's proposal to create phonetic symbols for a national language of China.[23] The experts agreed on the need for a national means of communication, but not on the symbols to be used or the sounds they should represent. Some suggested the Peking dialect, others preferred the tongues spoken in Chekiang-Kiangsu or Canton. The conference finally agreed on an eclectic selection of thirty-nine symbols—the National Phonetic Alphabet [*Chu-yin tzu-mu*], but not on the sounds to be represented by these symbols. Eventually, supporters of the Peking dialect won the disagreement. From the beginning, Ts'ai had preferred a system based on the Latin alphabet, presumably to facilitate the transition to Esperanto and the learning of European languages. Although he was brought to support the National Phonetic Alphabet, he was not in favor of using the Peking dialect as a base. Making the national language out of any local dialect, he believed, would alienate other areas, and he suggested that the vernacular, which lacked particular geographical connotations, would be the best solution.[24] At the request of the conference to promote the National Phonetic Alphabet, the ministry appropriated money, but little was accomplished during the postrevolutionary period.

During the new culture period, however, language reform was discussed in progressive journals throughout the Republic. A National Language Study Society was eventually established to reconsider the question, but government support to resolve the issue was not forthcoming. Wu Chih-hui, who had developed a set of phonetic symbols to replace the ancient ideographs, suggested that the vernacular language of eastern and northern China be used as a basis of the written language until an international language such as Esperanto could be introduced.[25] But Wu's suggestion was merely one of a multitude of such proposals floating aimlessly in the intellectual atmosphere of the new culture period.

A related problem was the simplification of written Chinese in order to facilitate the abolishment of illiteracy in China. Since the beginning of the century, educators had been aware of the need to bring literary expression closer to the spoken language. A few journals had switched to the use of the vernacular, but the controversy became heated when Hu Shih took a position under Ts'ai Yüan-p'ei at Peking University and recommended the use of vernacular Chinese in place of the traditional literary language as the basic written language of the nation. He was joined by Peking University etymologist Ch'ien Hsüan-t'ung who insisted that the Confucian system could not be destroyed until the language of its expression had been done away with. Although the literary language [wen-yen] was more elegant as a means of expression, it was extremely difficult to learn. Consequently, a Chinese could not read the written language without special training, even if he knew the character equivalents in the vernacular. For Hu, the new culture had to be a mass culture, and that meant the use of the vernacular as a means of expression in literature.

Ts'ai, as chancellor, permitted opponents of the *pai-hua* movement to teach at the university, but he favored the progressive movement's attempt to simplify the written language. He was convinced that the vernacular would be dominant in the future. First, it was the contemporary language, and he felt that new ideas should be expressed through contemporary means. If the literary language—the language of the ancients—was used to express modern ideas, then a certain amount of time would be lost in translation, and for no good purpose.

Secondly,

> our ancestors had no other courses to study than the national language. From age six to age 20, all that one wrote and read was the language of the ancients, so it was easy to learn. Now there is much science that needs to be studied, and if we do not cut down on the time needed to study the national language, how will we manage? Besides, in the past only a small minority learned to read, and in their environment if they wasted a little time, what difference did it make? Today we want all the people to be able to read and write, so how can we ask them to waste time?[26]

Ts'ai called upon the example of the European Renaissance to prove his point. Latin, the European equivalent of China's literary language, had dominated until the Renaissance. Then Europeans began to use their local languages in order to save time in expressing ideas.

Characteristically, Ts'ai did not want to entirely eliminate the literary language, which would always have some use as poetry or in describing art. For ordinary writing, however, and in most forms of literary expression in modern China, the vernacular would dominate. In his own writing, Ts'ai attempted to demonstrate this distinction. He wrote mainly in the vernacular, but when he wrote about art, literature, or philosophy, he resorted to the literary style. Most of his writing was more literary in tone than the conscious colloquialism of Hu Shih, but less literary than the style of most of his colleagues who probably felt that their educational level would be judged by the elegance of their written style. There is no denying that the vernacular movement had considerable success during this period. Led by Lu Hsün, a new school of writers arose who used the vernacular as their means of expression and in their writing as well, where the lives of everyday Chinese became increasingly the subject of their work. Journals which before 1919 had been almost entirely in the literary language changed over quickly to the new medium. The movement also effected teaching; in January 1920, the Ministry of Education announced that the vernacular would soon be used at the elementary levels in all primary schools in China.[27]

There were other ways of attempting to reach those who were not in school. Ts'ai had been turning his attention to this problem since 1912, when he and his friends from the *New Century,* Li Shih-tseng and Wu Chih-hui, set up the Frugal Study Society for Chinese students in France [*Liu-fa Chien-hsüeh-hui*]. It encouraged young Chinese to study abroad through grants of financial assistance. With Ts'ai's help, a language training institute was established in Peking, and from 1912 to 1913, several students were sent to France in this manner. Unfortunately, Yüan Shih-k'ai's pressure forced the program to be disbanded.[28]

When the First World War began, there was a need in France for laborers to work in factories. The founders of the society saw this as an opportunity to develop their scheme, and in June 1915 they started the Association for Diligent Work and Frugal Study [*Ch'in-kung Chien-hsüeh-hui*] in Paris.[29] Schools to train high school graduates in language were opened throughout China. Students were expected to devote part of their time in France to study, and part in working in factories for the war effort. Later, the Sino-French Educational Association [*Hua-fa Chiao-yü-hui*] was formed to facilitate the exchange of students and promote Franco-Chinese friendship.[30] Ts'ai took charge of the program until he returned to China in late 1916. From some points of view, the program was successful—several hundred Chinese students had broadened their experience with study and work in France. Eventually, however, the school split between advocates of Kropotkin and followers of Karl Marx, and the program disintegrated amid mutual recriminations. The example of the society earned considerable attention in China, however, and ultimately stimulated the formation of similar anarchist organizations.[31]

The Emancipation of Women. A related problem was the issue of female emancipation. Ts'ai had become closely involved in promoting female education since his early days in Shanghai, when he set up the Patriotic Girls' School. According to Ts'ai, he had developed his ideas of sex equality from reading Chinese literature, and grew to dislike the classics' emphasis on female inferiority. He carried this concern for women's rights into the republican period where he took an active role in promoting the development of coeducational schools and other improvements for women. Some minor changes had taken place during the final years of the old dynasty, and Ts'ai had proposed broadening educational opportunities for women during his brief tenure as minister of education in 1912. However, the actual changes achieved in female education in the early Republic were minimal. Slightly over 4 percent of all elementary school students in early republican China were girls, and none attended institutions above the lower middle-school level.[32]

Female emancipation attracted considerable concern during the new culture period, sparked by articles on woman's growing role in Western society, and by stories of Western women such as Ibsen's Nora and Hedda. Ts'ai became an active champion of the female cause in the young Republic. His greatest contribution was in the realm of higher education. In 1920, women were admitted to Peking University for the first time, when Ts'ai pointed out that the rules did not prohibit their admission. By 1923, there were more than one hundred female students in major Chinese institutes of higher learning. Ts'ai's position was that female inferiority in China was due to historical causes only, and that women were then showing that they were equal to and in some aspects even superior to men.[33] It was necessary, however, to change woman's outlook on life, which until then had been limited to being a good wife and mother. This change could be accomplished by granting women greater economic independence, political equality, and educational opportunities. In this way they would be able to abandon their dependence on men and their overriding concern for clothes and wealth.

Ts'ai did not deny the importance of marriage and motherhood. A good wife helps to make a good husband and can make her sons and daughters good citizens. In his view, it was illogical to feel that the capabilities of women stopped there. Man's active strength is wasted if just applied to one family. Therefore, a mother who can teach her own children and grandchildren should consider the possibility of entering teaching, in order to teach other children as well.[34]

Ts'ai's position, then, was to grant women the additional right of finding an identity beyond their domestic obligations. With the extended family system in China still in existence, Ts'ai recognized the difficulty of emancipating women, so he advocated the abolition of the big family system and the institution of marriage itself. Although his activities in this regard had minimal success, his educational endeavors were generally successful. As minister of education in 1912, he had promoted coeducation at the elementary level. By 1928, Ts'ai had obtained full equality for women in the Chinese educational system.[35]

The qualities of the New Culture Movement—a profound humanism, a tinge of moralism, an intense desire to move toward the ultimate utopia—find perhaps their best expression in the beliefs of Ts'ai Yüan-p'ei. True, Ts'ai was riding a tiger. The emotions that he and his fellow intellectuals had aroused over the preceding decade were too violent to be held in check for long. If the prescriptions he offered did not take immediate effect, his audience would turn to other nostrums.

It is not surprising that Ts'ai and Peking University became the target of attack from conservative elements in China which opposed the New Culture Movement. Although he was not the most radical of the intellectuals in China, Ts'ai held the position of highest trust in society. It seemed as if he were using his position to protect the other radicals who were sniping at the traditional system from under his wing at the university. At first, this attack from the right was not organized, and came from disgruntled literati who feared the destruction of their classics and the literary language. Some of the opposition to the new movement occurred within the university—by conservative stalwarts such as Liu Shih-p'ei and Ku Hung-ming. The main antagonist outside Peita was Lin Shu (Chin-nan), a translator of Western works but a supporter of the literary language and the Confucian classics. Lin had been attacked by many of the reformers and was goaded into making a public counterattack. He wrote short stories in which the leading reformers, Hu, Ch'en, and Ts'ai, were ridiculed and portrayed as pompous fools.[36] While not approving of the New Culture Movement and the protection it received from the university administration, the government felt no need to intervene directly in the conflict. However, the security of the government became jeopardized as the movement gathered strength. Aimless social and intellectual resentment turned on the source of policy, the central government in Peking.

In March 1919, an exchange of letters took place which symbolized the issues of the controversy. Lin Shu wrote a letter to Ts'ai in which he charged that the reformers were attempting to destroy the very basis of Chinese society, the social structure, the Confucian ethical values, and the literary language. He stated that reformers in China had been asking the nation to change its ways since the late Ch'ing dynasty. Despite all the reforms that had been implemented, China had not become strong. Destruction of tradition would only destroy Chinese civilization itself.

Ts'ai's reply defended the university against the accusations in Lin's letter.[37] He denied that instructors were teaching the students to discard the Chinese classics or Confucian ethical doctrines. The university, he said, did not dictate to members of the faculty what they should advocate outside the classroom, which was none of its business. The only limitation on their expression of ideas within the classroom was that what they advocate can be rationally maintained. He denied that those instructors, such as Hu Shih, who were exposing the classics to scientific analysis, were critical of Confucius or his doctrines. The Association for Confucian Religion was doing more harm to Confucian thought by wrongly asserting that it was a religion.[38]

Replying to Lin's charge that the university was assisting in the destruction of traditional ethics, Ts'ai stated that the university had encouraged the establishment of the Society for the Promotion of Virtue, many of whose standards were even higher than those of Confucius. He also denied that university policies had contributed to the destruction of the literary language, pointing out that almost all of the school textbooks were written in the literary style. In conclusion, Ts'ai defended the university policy of allowing freedom of expression for all rational ideas even though they may contradict the views of the day.

Both letters were highly publicized at the time, and Ts'ai's response became one of the primary documents of the new thought movement, exemplifying the ideals of the younger generation at Peking University and elsewhere. It was effectively written, disarming many of the criticisms that Lin Shu had incorporated in his own letter. Nevertheless, it is also true, as Chow Tse-tsung has pointed out, that on a number of points Ts'ai avoided the issue or indulged in self-contradiction.[39] First, although he denied that instructors were teaching students to abandon the old literature or traditional culture, it was virtually impossible for men of strong views, as most reformers were, to teach without making their students aware of their ideals. It is unlikely that they would shrink from advocating these ideas in their classes, particularly in view of the reformist conviction that change must come through education and propaganda. If Ch'en Tu-hsiu was anxious to have his views on literature and democracy known through his articles in *New Youth,* is it possible that he would avoid advocating the same views in his classes? From Ch'en's viewpoint, he would be guilty of almost criminal negligence if he did not seek to persuade his students to share his views. Ts'ai was being unrealistic or dishonest in claiming that such ideas were not espoused at the university.

Secondly, he evaded the ethical issue by bringing up the Society for the Promotion of Virtue. No Confucian would deny that the strictures of the society, with the possible exception of avoiding government service, could be considered moral from a Confucian point of view. It was also true, however, that among Confucian values were many not covered by the standards set by the society, particularly with regard to family and society relationships, standards being harshly attacked by many society members. Lin Shu must have laughed at Ts'ai's contention that university reformers such as Ch'en Tu-hsiu did not advocate changes such as female emancipation, the destruction of the traditional clan system, and rules of filial piety. Ts'ai was justified in indicating that Confucian values were not the only possible ethical values, but he is open to the charge of evading the issue raised in Lin's letter.

Finally, in his reply, Ts'ai justified the inclusion of supporters of monarchy and feudalism such as Ku Hung-ming and Liu Shih-p'ei by stating that they were teaching in positions (i.e., Chinese and English literature respectively) in which they were not likely to discuss politics. Despite his defense of freedom of speech for all opinions which can be rationally held, he tacitly admitted that the political views of monarchists and defenders of the old political and social order should not be directly espoused in political science courses at the university. He mentioned elsewhere that ideas eliminated by natural selection should not be propagated. By this, of course, he implied that such ideas as monarchy and feudalism had been eliminated by natural selection. Such a contention is obviously a potential infringement of freedom of speech, since it requires a subjective view of natural selection. It resembles the contention in Communist states that capitalist and bourgeois concepts of liberal democracy and individualism are outmoded and harmful to society, and that they have been eliminated by social progress. It is interesting to note, in view of Ts'ai's reputation as defender of free thought, that his vaunted concept, at least in this case, was limited to thought, and not to expression in class.[40]

In any case, the conservatives in early 1919 continued their attacks on Peita and its chancellor, some even suggesting that the parliament, controlled by the warlord regime, attempt to impeach Ts'ai on the charge of treasonable behavior. General Hsü Shu-cheng became so angry that he threatened to bomb the university and its defiant chancellor. The government was trimming, however, and the bill to impeach did not succeed.

The conservatives had good reason to indict Ts'ai for traitorous behavior toward traditional culture. Led by university intellectuals, public opinion in Peking and elsewhere grew more radical and more concerned with the political situation. There was increasing, if superficial, concern for the poor and the uneducated, and student organizations sprang into existence with work-study schemes and similar activities. The steam pressure was building up, and any issue was likely to blow the lid off the political situation.

6

May Four and After

The unquenchable optimism of the new culture period was based, above all, on faith in the West—faith in the powers of science, in the qualities of democracy, and in Dewey, Ibsen, Kropotkin, and Woodrow Wilson. Curiously, the First World War did not have an immediate effect on Chinese confidence in Western civilization. Essays and articles appearing in progressive journals during the last months of the war indicate that many Chinese intellectuals still believed in the Western model and hoped that the war would unlock the gates to world progress. Few, like Li Ta-chao, in an article written in *New Youth*, stated that the war signaled the decline of the Western liberal democracies and the rise of Bolshevik power.[1] Many, however, welcomed the victory of the Entente powers as proof that democracy and open diplomacy had triumphed over authoritarianism and militarism.

Ts'ai, who had been in Europe during the war, attempted to keep the war from creating in China a crisis of confidence. In a speech celebrating the end of the war in November, he maintained that the war had released great forces in human civilization. Referring to the title of his address, "The Interaction of the Forces of Light and Darkness" [Hei-an yü kuang-ming ti hsiao-chang], he stated that the progress of evolution resembled the ancient Zoroastrian polarity of light and darkness, good and evil.[2] In the war, the four forces of darkness (Might makes right, conspiracy, dictatorship, racism) had been overcome by the forces of light (Mutual Aid, justice, democracy, internationalism). To clarify the final point, he asserted that Germany had preached the "White Man's Burden," whereas the Entente united all races in the struggle against the Central Powers. Just as the French Revolution had brought an end to political inequality in France, the result of the war would be the extinction of social inequality throughout the world.

In this and similar addresses, Ts'ai displayed an overwhelming confidence in Western civilization. Under other circumstances, he might have been able to transmit his optimism to his countrymen. But the seeds of change were soon apparent; great hopes often lead to great disappointments, and there is no denying the disillusion of educators when the Western powers betrayed Chinese trust at Versailles in 1919. Hope gave way to anger and cynicism. Perhaps Ts'ai did a disservice to his own cause by raising hopes too high. Clearly, the award of Chinese territory to Japan as the spoils of war did not symbolize to China the victory of the forces of light in the world.

The anger and frustration over China's continuing distress were only awaiting an opportunity to overflow into widespread disorder. By mid-1918, some progressives were becoming increasingly restive because of China's problems. Ch'en Tu-hsiu's reaction was symptomatic. In the 15 July 1918 issue of *New Youth*, he abandoned his pledge to abjure politics, claiming that all bets were off when China's survival was at stake.[3] Students themselves became restless and started to organize. When one group founded the highly nationalist *Kuo-min tsa-chih* [National Review] to express their feelings, Ts'ai Yüan-p'ei praised them for coming to the defense of the homeland. Ironically, in a preface to the opening issue of the review, he told them to maintain their faith in internationalism.[4]

The issue over Japan's position in Shantung Province occurred at this time and became the immediate issue which caused the May Four demonstrations, although another issue might have done just as well. When the participants at the Versailles Peace Conference agreed that Japan should be granted Germany's former rights in North China, the Chinese became disgusted with the Western democracies. China, like Japan, had fought on the side of the allies, hoping to achieve a better bargaining position to rid herself of the unequal treaties. Instead, to reward the Japanese for their meager part in the war, the treaties were perpetuated. The evident willingness of the Chinese government to acquiesce in the decision increased resentment. Frustrated in their desire to attack Japan and the West, students and intellectuals focused their resentment on the government in Peking. On 4 May 1919, students from Peita and other local institutions demonstrated and caused damage in the capital. As a result, several participants were arrested. The students were joined by other elements of society in their protest against the Versailles Treaty, including many intellectual and political leaders of the nation. Resistance to Japanese demands was a point that almost all Chinese could agree on, regardless of their ideological persuasion. Even Lin Shu shared the distaste for a Japanese occupation of Chinese territory. Consequently, a boycott of Japanese goods developed as merchants and workers in China's major cities joined the protest movement.

When news of the student arrests spread throughout the capital, a mass student meeting was held to discuss future action. As chancellor of the foremost university in Peking, Ts'ai had earlier indicated his dislike of student demonstrations. In 1918, student riots had taken place despite his attempt to restrain them, and as a result he had submitted his resignation.[5] Ts'ai was dissuaded from carrying out his intention, however, and made it clear that the students should devote their time to studies, not to political organization and activism. On the evening of 4 May, Ts'ai addressed a meeting of students and exerted a calming influence:

> This patriotic movement is something that is occurring in all countries these days, and is nothing to be concerned about. You have gone a little far today, and you should not forget that in saving the nation you should not forget to study. . . . Still, people's rights should be protected, and I intend to demand that the government release the arrested students within three days. . . .[6]

Ts'ai concluded that he would take responsibility for the affair, on the condition that the students return to classes. Ts'ai's relaxed manner was contagious, and the participants agreed to give him an opportunity to settle the matter through negotiation.

When Ts'ai attempted to discuss the problem with the chief of police, he was unsuccessful, and new meetings took place the next day, opening a student strike. Ts'ai and the heads of other local educational institutions tried once more to obtain the students' release. This attempt was eventually successful, and the students were finally freed on 7 May. Despite achieving his immediate ends, Ts'ai was depressed by the whole affair, partly because of the government's distasteful attitude throughout the crisis, and also because he feared that the students would continue using the "miracle method" of demonstrations to obtain their goals.[7] His own views had undergone a change from his revolutionary days, when violence and assassination did not bother him so long as laudable goals were involved. He had now become an apostle of moderation and evolutionary change, and he could no longer reconcile admirable ends with violent means.

The incident had a predictable effect on conservative and pro-Japanese elements, many of whom blamed Ts'ai for the events. Demands arose to close the university and dismiss the chancellor, and rumors spread that Ts'ai would be assassinated. On 9 May, after leaving a note of resignation on his desk at the office, Ts'ai left the city and retired to Hangchow in central China. As he traveled south, he sent a public letter to the students at Peita, stating that although he believed that the student protests were based on sincere patriotism, he had to resign as chancellor because he had accepted final responsibility for their behavior. His resignation, he explained, was not caused by the students' actions.[8] In a telegram to the president of the Republic, the premier, and the minister of education, he stated that the unfortunate behavior of the students was his responsibility and asked that the government take a broad view and understand their doltish actions.

The students themselves were concerned that Ts'ai would be replaced by a chancellor who would represent the conservative elements in society, and there was great pressure in intellectual circles for him to return. Although the government refused to accept Ts'ai's resignation, he insisted on remaining away from Peking.[9] Eventually, the government was forced to accept most of the students' demands; three ministers connected with the treaty decision were dismissed, the Chinese delegates in Paris refused to ratify the treaty, and charges against the students were dropped. In September, Ts'ai returned to his post in Peking on condition that the university be permitted to maintain its own discipline.[10]

It is generally agreed that Ts'ai was one of the three or four Chinese most responsible for the conditions causing the May Four incident. It is also true that his attitude toward the incident and its ramifications was somewhat equivocal. His belief in education and gradualism had grown over the years, and he seemed to feel that violence served no useful purpose in republican China. He told Chiang Monlin that "he had never intended to incite the students to revolt, but that in demonstrating they had acted on patriotic impulses which could hardly be condemned."[11] He shared the general feeling of disgust that the government had submitted to Japanese demands, but he was emotionally repelled by the specter of violence and revolution which the protest movement had unleashed. He also feared that the growth of a radical movement in Chinese universities could have a detrimental effect on learning. In July, he addressed an open letter to the students in which he told them: "You have aroused the people and they have all supported you. There is nothing to criticize you for in this. Still, as for you as individuals, do you want to limit yourself to this contribution forever? And forget the important responsibilities which you have sacrificed to protect?"[12] A more important obligation, he told them, was to their studies. European influence began in the 1860s, and China's first reaction was to strengthen her defenses. Then she realized the need for political reform. Finally, China saw the need for education, for specialized technology, for mass literacy, and for people to be trained in all aspects of modern knowledge. What was needed, he said, was not to arouse the people again. They had been aroused, and you cannot go back and do it all over again. Since the nation was conscious of its needs, what it required was greater knowledge, high-minded leaders, and improved manufactures. Students alone, he said, could give China these qualities. Commenting on the political concerns of the students, Ts'ai said that they should not expect immediate perfection. Politics is a complex profession and nothing is ever finally realized. The primary obligation of students, he said, was to return to their studies. Those over twenty-one years of age who wished to participate in politics could do so, but they should not involve the university.[13]

Later, Ts'ai tried to put the incident in perspective, maintaining that the government was primarily to blame for the violence of the movement. When Ku Hung-ming and Lin Shu called the results of May Four the action of "floods and wild beasts," Ts'ai retorted in an article with the same name [Hung-shui yü meng-shou], in which he compared the new thought movement to a flood which had to sweep away the old and could eventually be channeled into useful purposes. The wild beasts were the warlords in Peking who had to be swept away in the torrent.[14] By trying to dam up the flood, instead of guiding it, the government had made the incident of May Four inevitable.

The Deepening Crisis. The May Four incident ushered in a new era in the history of modern China, yet it did not signal the end of the New Culture Movement. As one student of the period pointed out, 1919 represents a watershed between the first and the second phase of the movement.[15] If the first phase from 1915 to 1919 was characterized by optimism, faith in Western democracy, confidence in the efficacy of education and peaceful cultural reform, the second phase, following 4 May, was more strident, less imbued with humanist democracy, and more prone to political action and violence.

This new trend is not immediately noticeable in the written material concerning the period. As late as the winter of 1919, *New Youth* issued a manifesto which allegedly represented the views of the entire New Youth Society, the basic elements of which were Mutual Aid, human-itarianism, universal love, democracy, science, and trust in the moral progress of mankind.[16] When the American philosopher John Dewey visited China in 1919 and 1920, he found considerable support for his suggestions that the construction of a modern society in China be based on gradualism and the principles of liberal democracy.

Beneath the surface, however, a new mood was being generated among the progressive forces. Skepticism over the effectiveness of Western democracy and a tendency to rely on political action, not education, accompanied the change. In part, the reaction against the West was a consequence of the Western powers' decision at Versailles to grant Chinese territory to Japan. That decision questioned the optimistic forecasts of Ts'ai and others that the armistice signaled the end of secret diplomacy, injustice, and racism in society. But the trend away from democracy was deeper than that—it had begun before the May Four incident, with Ch'en's decision to undertake political action, with Li Ta-chao's growing interest in the Bolshevik experiment in Russia, and with the growing impatience throughout the movement over the failure of gradualism to realize social reforms.

The primary recipient of the new mood was communism. If Chinese intellectuals had looked to the West as the only suitable model for the construction of a new China, the Soviet experiment of 1917 indicated that liberal democracy and utopian socialism were not the only roads to social change. The Chinese intellectuals who turned to Bolshevism did not have to abandon democracy. They simply had to abandon the voluntarist, gradualist approach taken by Western liberalism in favor of the collectivist and revolutionary approach of Bolshevism, the utopian and libertarian approach of anarchism for the Marxist-Leninist emphasis on revolutionary discipline and social mobilization. Those Chinese who sought national revival and were reluctant to sacrifice national unity for individual liberty preferred Marxist ideas over Western liberalism or anarchism. By emphasizing the strength of the nation-state through the collective will of the populace—mobilization of the population in order to realize social goals—Marxism showed an ability to satisfy a yearning held by the progressive community.

Political radicalism was not the only beneficiary of May Four. Not the least of the social forces active in the early 1920s was a rising backlash against the thrust for Westernization and social change in the early republican period. Led by erstwhile reformers such as Liang Ch'i-ch'ao and Yen Fu, conservative forces drew strength from the agony of the West in World War I and stated that the materialistic virtues of the West had led to holocaust and social revolution. After returning from a visit to postwar Europe, Liang emphasized that China should reject Western materialism and rely more on her own spiritual sources. Liang had not abandoned his admiration for liberalism, and he did not counsel China to turn away from all aspects of the West. However, he denounced social Darwinism as the cause of the agony of World War I.

In a way, China was becoming simultaneously more conservative and more radical. This was probably a consequence of the polarization of opinion created by the events surrounding May Four and represented the development of a situation in which the humanist-oriented urban intelligentsia would increasingly find themselves attacked from both sides. The intellectual journals under moderate leadership spoke with authority about trends and events in Western Europe and the United States, and they continued to attract a readership in the Westernized urban areas of China. Nevertheless, forces were at work in China inexorably drawing support away from humanist solutions.

Warlord Politics, Democratic Education. The May Four period had exerted little immediate influence on the nature of politics in Peking. Seemingly oblivious to the changes taking place in the nation as a whole, the warlords continued to conduct a sterile game of musical chairs. As the meaningless charade continued into the 1920s, the arguments on behalf of democracy, gradualism, and nonviolence, calling for patience and a reliance on educational reform, began to seem threadbare. Indeed, the moderate progressives such as Ts'ai and Hu Shih found it difficult to exert any influence on the government. Ever since the May Four demonstrations ended, warlords, contemptuous of democratic principles and ruthless in their taxation of the peasantry, had engaged in flagrant disregard of the constitution, the principles of republican government, and the welfare of the people. On several occasions Ts'ai had wanted to resign. However, out of a sense of duty to his students and a desire to protect the school from politicians, he decided to stay. By the spring of 1922, he had reluctantly agreed that the situation was getting out of control. At his suggestion, Hu Shih drew up a public letter to be signed by a number of prominent educators and public figures and to be published in Hu's journal *The Struggle Weekly* [Nu-li chou-pao].[17] The manifesto, as Grieder pointed out, was liberal in tone. It noted the widespread abuses committed by the government and called for political reforms—for honesty in government and a greater concern for the public welfare. Recognizing that past attempts to persuade the warlord regime to change its ways had failed, the manifesto urged concerned citizens to force the government to convene a reunification assembly to unite the North with Sun's military regime in the South, to reduce military expenditures and to cleanse the bureaucracy of the corruption which had reached perilous levels. Rebuking those humanist intellectuals who had reacted to 4 May by turning in despair to their own private interests, the manifesto stated that "good men" should not resign and leave total power to the corrupt elements in society, but should take a firm stand and develop a fighting spirit to force the government to reform itself. Not surprisingly, the petition brought forth little response from the government. Nor did it persuade many "good men" to enter the political arena.

The weakness of the liberals in influencing government actions was illustrated by the Lo Wen-kan incident. On 18 November 1922, Lo, the minister of finance, was arrested at the instigation of elements within the government under the pretext of an abuse of authority. He was kept in jail for two months without evidence of his guilt being furnished, and in January 1923 he was released for lack of evidence. Four days later, Minister of Education P'eng Yün-i arranged to have him rearrested without furnishing any evidence of his guilt. Evidently, P'eng had done this to please Lo's enemies in parliament. Ts'ai, much of the faculty at Peking University, and the students were outraged by the illegality of the proceedings. Convinced that the "good men" were not going to emerge from their studies, Ts'ai submitted his resignation as chancellor of the university. He offered the following explanation from Tientsin:

> It is said in the *Book of Changes* that the man of no principle knows only how to advance, not to retreat. In recent years we have been living in confused circumstances because of such men of small principle who do not know when to retreat. The action of resignation is not just a negative action to avoid unpleasantness, but can indirectly exert a positive influence.[18]

Ts'ai's resignation reopened an old chapter in his approach to adversity. Although an anarchist, he had not, since 1912, accepted the anarchist prohibition against government service, taking the position that good men should not shrink from doing their duty, no matter how unpleasant such a chore might become. On this basis, Ts'ai had accepted the chancellorship of Peking University although the government was in the hands of unsavory elements. But now, he continued in his resignation statement, the latest actions of the government have been too scandalous. As chancellor, Ts'ai was obliged to deal with Minister P'eng on a daily basis, and since he felt that P'eng was responsible for the deplorable situation, he realized that he had to resign. His resignation was meant to symbolize his disgust with conditions in Peking, "where laws are tampered with, elections are purchased, truth and falsehood are matters of no consequence, but private advantage and profit are matters of importance. The bad odor of Peking [is] daily becoming more noxious and I have felt that I [cannot] bear it any longer."

Because of Ts'ai's action, students and professors demonstrated against the minister of education and demanded that his resignation not be accepted, but the protesters were driven off. The agitation continued, however, growing into a nation-wide student protest and resulting in the fall of the cabinet and the release of Lo Wen-kan. Ts'ai's resignation was refused by the government, and he agreed to remain in his position. Because of the Fengtien-Chihli struggle, he asked for leave in July 1923 in order to take an extended tour of Europe.[19]

Ts'ai's resignation aroused a certain amount of interest in intellectual circles in China, but it did not spark a series of mass resignations. Ch'en Tu-hsiu, by now an active member of the Communist party, criticized Ts'ai's action as a negative approach to the problem. What the people needed, he believed, was a type of positive action to enable them to resist the warlord government. Ts'ai's attitude may be appropriate for scholars and bureaucrats, he said, but hardly for the common people. Hu Shih, who had earlier preached passive resistance, defended Ts'ai and maintained that his action would make the nation become more aware of its present deplorable condition. First, he said, you have to persuade men to stop behaving like swine, and then you can get rid of a swinish government. Ts'ai's resignation, therefore, provided a good example for individual action.[20]

For most educators, the consequences of the May Four period were promising and disconcerting. In one sense, the prospect for education was a depressing one. The student movement, stimulated by its influence during the hectic days of 1919, began a tradition of student activism which would carry over into succeeding decades. Students played an increasing role in politics and in school as well, where they were more prone to criticize their instructors, the curricula, and the administration. Occasionally, they translated their resentment into action. Evidently, student activism caused many educators to become pessimistic about the future of education in China at that time. Ts'ai's attempts to persuade the students at Peita to return to their studies were generally futile. He seemed to have lost his calming influence on the students, and on a few occasions, radical elements invaded his office to demand changes in university policy.[21]

On the other hand, the trend toward a more democratic system of education intensified during the years following May Four. Through the influence of John Dewey and his disciples, Chinese education began to feel the impact of the American system—in curricula, administration, and educational standards. Ts'ai became increasingly affected by Dewey's ideas, and although some of his educational goals differed from those of the American-trained educators, on most issues Ts'ai and the Deweyites were working in alliance. In 1922 they were rewarded when the Peking Ministry of Education promulgated a new system of education. The new reforms, sweeping in content, did not have a great impact on schools in China. Few provinces in China were under the control of the Peking regime, and since military requirements were given a higher priority, lack of money kept the educational system in a state of financial crisis.[22] To the Deweyites, however, education in China was moving in the right direction.

In the new system, the influence of Dewey and of Ts'ai Yüan-p'ei was marked.[23] The American credit system, the three-level approach for elementary and secondary education, was adopted, and more attention was given to vocational education and mass literacy. Emphasis was placed on the development of the individual, not on the adaptation of the individual to the needs of the state. Course materials emphasized the responsibilities of citizenship and humanitarianism rather than encouraging a strong nationalist spirit and resentment of foreigners. For that purpose, religion and political influence were minimized. The ultimate aim of the program was to foster democracy, individuality, and the creation of a progressive society. Although no specific educational standard was declared, five principles were set forth: democracy, the needs of society, individual character, the strengthening of the national economy, and local initiative.

A major problem in Chinese education during the period immediately following May Four was, from Ts'ai's point of view, the extent of Christian religious influence through missionary schools. Chinese nationalists had been attempting to limit the influence of Christian schools in China since the early 1900s, but with little success. There were several reasons for Chinese dissatisfaction over Christian influence in education—nationalism, concern that the schools developed in their students qualities detrimental to national unity, opposition to religious education of all kinds, and a desire that all education be under the direction of the government.[24] Regulations issued by the Chinese government against the spread of Christian education had been ineffective, however, and in the early twenties, nationalist groups formed a movement to attack the influence of Christianity in Chinese education.

In April 1922, the antireligious movement reached a crescendo with the formation of the Great Federation of Nonreligionists [Fei-tsung-chiao T'ung-meng Ta-yün-tung].[25] The movement was a consequence of a Christian youth meeting which took place at Tsinghua College in Peking in the same month. Influenced by the meeting, a Shanghai student group formed the Shanghai Great Federation of Non-religionists to oppose the activities of the Christian youth in Peking. A similar organization sprang up in Peking and held a mass meeting at the university. In his address to the group, Ts'ai was strongly critical of Christian influence in China.

He had become interested in the movement opposing the Christian religion in China, having contributed occasional articles to *Young China* [Shao-nien Chung-kuo], a journal run by the society of the same name which had become a focal point of antireligious sentiment.[26] In 1922, in an article entitled "The Independence of Education" [Chiao-yü tu-li-i], Ts'ai pointed out the incompatibility between religion and education, stating that religion was retrogressive by nature, whereas education was progressive.[27] The aim of teaching, he said, is to develop the intellectual faculties and perfect the dignity of a human being, "to render him capable of becoming an element in the evolution of humanity. It is not to mold him, like a vase, according to a preconceived plan. . . ." Public education should be exclusively in the hands of public instructors who can guarantee their purity of intention. Otherwise, he feared that science would be subordinate to religious doctrine, and mutual understanding and knowledge of the nature of the universe would inevitably suffer.

During his speech at the mass meeting, Ts'ai criticized the Christian system of schools in China. Since religion was an integral part of the curriculum at these schools, students were given little opportunity to acquaint themselves with Chinese culture.[28] Opposing all forms of religious influence in education, he proposed three principles: Faculties of theology should not be permitted to exist in higher education; religion could be taught within the Department of Philosophy, and a chair for the history of religions could be established for instruction in comparative religion. Religious propaganda should not be permitted in any school in China, nor should cults or prayers be allowed. And no one officially connected with a religious organization should have a voice in matters relating to education.

These were strong sentiments, of course, and they created considerable resistance. Many critics stated that he was opposing freedom of religious belief, but Ts'ai retorted that the movement only wanted to establish freedom *not* to believe in a religious faith. Although the results of the 1922 confrontation were inconclusive, they attracted nation-wide attention, and the antireligious sentiment of the early twenties began to crystallize into anti-Christian feeling, culminating in anti-Christian incidents during the Northern Expedition in 1926 and 1927. Eventually, the movement became more nationalistic and found support among many groups which were not antireligious as such. Major attacks on religious schools took place during the Nanking period, ending in the establishment of regulations forcing all private schools to comply with government standards. Religion was forbidden to be a mandatory subject, attendance at religious services could not be required, and the number of foreigners on the faculty of private schools was restricted. Opposition to Christianity for religious reasons allied with the general sentiment against Western influence, causing a gradual decrease in the influence of mission schools in China. Curiously, however, an immediate result of the 1922 movement was a backlash. The Mission Book Company reported that in the years following 1922, it sold an unprecedented number of Bibles.[29]

The Decline of the Humanist Spirit. During the new decade, the Chinese cultural revival shifted into new channels, from peaceful reform to political violence, from mass spontaneity to party organization, from gradualism and education to political and social revolution. In the process, the basic idealism of the new culture years turned to frustration and increasing anger. Ts'ai's popularity suffered along with the general decline of humanism. He was more activist inclined, more prone to preach egalitarianism and to have a sense of the importance of the masses than most of his liberal contemporaries. In effect, Ts'ai did not give off the air of academe that characterized many of his moderate colleagues. Although he was still a mandarin figure, and the sense of elitism still clung to him, there was no doubting the depth of the intellectual and emotional commitment to humanity beating in his breast. Ts'ai was clearly a man who felt the tragedies of poverty, disease, and evil in human society. This, however, could not always be said about many of his liberal contemporaries.

In the years following the May Four events, however, Ts'ai's emotional commitment did not help him to retain his reputation in the progressive movement. His attempt to solve the problems of poverty and inequality through ethics, education, and aesthetics was, in the opinion of many radicals, too gradualist. His only response to bad government was appeal and, ultimately, resignation. Nevertheless, a policy of passive resistance could have been effective in an indirect way. Ts'ai's behavior focused attention, however briefly, on the corruption and lack of support of the government. Ts'ai, however, did not realize that such traditional tactics were not likely to move the government or young radicals. And resignation, by itself, was not an effective method of dealing with a corrupt regime.[30]

The final judgment on Ts'ai's actions during these years has to be mixed. His concern for reform is clear and cannot be faulted. His desire to restrict his activities to the field of education is not blameworthy in light of his dislike of active politics. By escaping to Europe, he was reacting as thousands of other decent men have reacted in similar circumstances. But his belief that passive resistance would have positive results is not wholly convincing, since he followed it up by escaping abroad. Even Hu Shih, who defended Ts'ai's decision against the criticism of Ch'en Tu-hsiu, conceded that at the most Ts'ai's passive resistance would make everyone a little uncomfortable in his conscience.[31] And his decision to seek a balm for his wounds in Europe might simply make others conclude that he couldn't stand the heat of the kitchen.

By the 1920s, many Chinese intellectuals were less receptive to cerebral theories calling for cautious change and voluntary sacrifice. The revolt against gradualism had seeped into the student body at Peking University. Ts'ai as chancellor had dedicated his career to a vision of the university in which students themselves would help to determine the nature of their education. By the early 1920s, students were demonstrating in the chancellor's office and demanding more rights and changes in university policy. These actions, no doubt, prompted his rage and indignation. Where he called for moderation and concern for freedom of the individual, radicals called for violence and the use of revolutionary power. As Ts'ai stated, arbitrary power was unhealthy, but who was going to put China's problems right without the use of limitless power? Man has yet to find an answer to that question. Ts'ai may have been right in the long run, but at the time, he could hardly escape the dilemma posed by Chinese conditions. The humanist rose looked pathetic in the setting of warlord China.

7

Elder Statesman

Ts'ai remained in Europe for three years, spending most of his time assisting Li Shih-tseng and Wu Chih-hui, his old anarchist colleagues, in running the Sino-French University [*Chung-Fa Ta-hsüeh*] in Lyons, France. In 1924, he went to London to help persuade the British to annul the Boxer Indemnity. Ts'ai's proposal was to establish a university in China which would train specialists in several fields, providing an intellectual cadre to staff the Chinese government in future years.[1] The money which had been earmarked for the Boxer Indemnity would be used to provide funds for the operation of the university.

In 1926, Ts'ai received a telegram from the Ministry of Education asking him to return to China, where he was still titular head of Peking University. The China that he returned to was changing. When he had left, the two competitors to the warlord regime, the Communist party and the Kuomintang, were almost as antipathetic to each other as to the warlords. Shortly after, in an attempt to tighten up party discipline and instill enthusiasm in the faction-ridden revolutionary organization, Sun Yat-sen had reorganized the Kuomintang and agreed to cooperate with the Communist party against the common enemy in Peking. Consequently, the reorganization of 1924, assisted by the Soviet adviser Michael Borodin, had moved Kuomintang policies to the left, and many of the party's conservative "old comrades" deserted or were expelled from the party, some drifting into the warlord-dominated Anfu clique.[2] Another group, although opposed to the leftward drift of the party, remained in the Kuomintang and called itself the Western Hills faction. Ts'ai, who had been appointed by Sun to membership in the Central Supervisory Committee [*Chung-yang Chien-ch'a Wei-yuan-hui*] in absentia, was not involved in these events; his relationship with Sun had apparently always been pleasant but formal. He had occasionally disagreed with Sun's policies, in particular his refusal to compromise with the Peking government, but he had been generally loyal to the ideas of the Kuomintang leader. In turn, Sun had frequently supported Ts'ai in party councils, defending his decision to accept the chancellorship of Peking University in 1917, and insisting on Ts'ai's appointment to high position in the reorganized party after 1924.[3]

When he returned to China in 1926, Ts'ai immediately became involved in activities against Sun Ch'uan-fang, who had been in control of Chekiang Province for several years. He also joined his anarchist friends Li Shih-tseng, Wu Chih-hui, and Chang Ching-chiang in a faction which came to be referred to as the *Genro,* or "Elder Statesmen."[4] The old anarchists had remained in the party after Sun's reorganization and held a controlling position in the new Central Supervisory Committee, which occupied an ambiguous position in the government political hierarchy.[5] It was responsible to the Central Executive Committee, but its counterpart in the Soviet Union, the Control Commission, had certain extra-hierarchical control and censorate powers, and its role was not clearly defined in China. During the succeeding events, the Elder Statesmen maintained an intermediate position between the radicals, who had been in general control of the party since the 1924 reorganization, and the right-wing Western Hills faction. The Elder Statesmen accepted Sun's policy of cooperation with the Chinese Communist party and alliance with the Soviet Union, but they were unprepared to follow the left-wing leadership in allowing a Communist ascendancy in the party, a danger which began to appear in 1926, after Sun's death.[6]

On his return to China, therefore, Ts'ai was to be directly involved in the controversy between the Kuomintang and the Communist party. Ts'ai's views on communism, like those of Sun himself, seem to have been ambivalent. His interest in the Communist ideal dated back to the early years of the century, and despite many years of admiration for Western civilization, he became convinced that European capitalism had resulted in a widening gap between rich and poor, and would eventually be superseded by a system which would provide equal opportunity for all. Capitalism emphasized selfishness and greed, not sacrifice and Mutual Aid. It is not surprising, therefore, that he considered capitalism to be part of the bones and seeds which China should spit out when assimilating Western values.

Yet Ts'ai's interest in communism never led him directly to Marxism. When the Bolsheviks began to apply the Marxist doctrine in Russia after the 1917 revolution, Ts'ai was distantly interested in the experiment and promoted the establishment of a Marxist Study Society at the university. In August 1922, Ts'ai attended a party welcoming the Soviety envoy Adolph Joffe to China, and toasted him:

> Since the penetration of European thought into China, a process of social, economic, and political change has developed in this country. The Chinese revolution was a political one. Now it is tending in the direction of a social revolution. Russia furnishes a good example to China, which thinks it advisable to learn the lessons of the Russian revolution which started also as a political revolution. Please accept the hearty welcome of the pupil to the teacher.[7]

Ts'ai's moderate eulogy to the Soviet experiment was probably after-dinner oratory, lubricated by a few glasses of *Shao-hsing* wine. Marxism, with its emphasis on progress through class conflict, could not appeal to Ts'ai, who instinctively preferred progress through a harmony of interests.

In any case, he could not see the relevance of the Marxist historical dialectic to rural and clan-oriented China. Shortly after the 30 May 1925 incident in Shanghai, which prompted many Europeans and Chinese to voice their fear of communism, Ts'ai retorted that Marxist class struggle would find little favor among the Chinese. The basis of Chinese philosophy, he reasoned, is the principle that excessive wealth and excessive poverty are wrong. Under the Chinese family system there is no primogeniture, and the parental estate descends equally to all the children, thus subdividing great fortunes within a few generations. Even custom requires the rich to share with the poor among their kin. In consequence, he maintained,

> In China the wealthy usually live almost as simply as the poor. For this reason the poor have seldom hated the rich. Although within the last dozen or so years great corporations and modern industrial establishments have grown up in China, antagonism between capital and labor is not yet strong. Measures developed in Europe and America for the protection of the working people are being adopted, and most of the new corporations are owned by a great number of shareholders. A concentration of capital in the hands of a great magnate is hardly to be feared.[8]

Ts'ai did not deny the potential popularity of communism, but he did not believe that the class struggle preached by Marx was appropriate in the Chinese setting. As we can see from hindsight, he ignored the potential force of Communist ideology in the rural areas where there was perhaps more resentment against the rich to be tapped than he realized. Ts'ai's comments illustrate the fact that Westerners were not the only ones who misunderstand the nature of the Chinese Revolution.

Immediately after arriving in China in February 1926, he made the following statement:

> The intellectuals of China must reconstruct the nation with the same zeal and devotion as the European intellectuals reconstructed their nations after the destruction of the war. The conditions in China, of course, are not exactly the same. One can only say in general that in the task of reconstruction, the Mutual Aid of Kropotkin will be of more value to us than the class struggle of Marx. We need not wait for the foreigners to do our work for us; let us Chinese reconstruct China ourselves.[9]

The events of 1926 and 1927 convinced Ts'ai that the Communist party was not the true representative of the Chinese Revolution. While Sun was alive, and the Soviet Union was the only major power willing to assist the Kuomintang, alliance with the Communist party was defensible. After Sun's death, however, the Communists began to promote their views more actively and organized their forces within the Kuomintang. Fortunately, Ts'ai felt, Chiang Kai-shek was not as blind to Communist activities as a number of other comrades (he probably had in mind Wang Ching-wei and other members of the party left wing) and had cut down Communist influence in the Canton coup of March 1926. Communist policies, Ts'ai felt, were only designed to "cheat the proletariat and the peasantry."[10] Although he had represented the progressive side of the reform movement during its entire existence, Ts'ai slowly came around to supporting the moderate elements in the party, and at times seemed allied to the right-wing Western Hills faction as well.

The split in the Kuomintang, which was created by Sun's reorganization and the rising hopes for success in unifying the country under the nationalist forces, widened in 1926 when the radicals, in control of the Central Executive Committee, moved from Canton to Wuhan where the Kuomintang had maintained its provisional government since 1917. In March 1927, the third session of the executive committee was held at Hankow. Communist influence, led by Ch'en Tu-hsiu and Borodin, was growing in the radical wing of the party and inspired distrust and resentment among moderates and conservatives who were fearful that China would lose control over its own revolution.[11] The majority at the session moved against Commander in Chief Chiang Kai-shek, who had boycotted the conference, dismissing him from his position. The moderates at the conference thereupon appealed to the Central Supervisory Committee, dominated by the Elder Statesmen, to reduce Communist influence in the party and restore control to the moderates. Conservatives felt that the committee could impeach members of the government at Hankow on charges of disloyalty to Sun Yat-sen's Three People's Principles.

Meanwhile, Wang Ching-wei, the leader of the left-wing faction of the party, had just returned from abroad and discussed the situation with Chiang Kai-shek and the Elder Statesmen in Shanghai. Chiang informed Wang that he could no longer cooperate with the Central Executive Committee because it had dismissed him from his post as commander in chief and was dominated by the Communists.[12] He demanded that the Communists be removed from the party and a new leadership established. Wu Chih-hui wanted the Central Supervisory Committee to make a unilateral decision to abandon the alliance with the Communists and undertake a campaign to cleanse the party. Wang disagreed, holding that all decisions of the committee had to be approved by the Central Executive Committee. He suggested that a fourth session of the executive committee be called to settle the problem between the two factions. On 10 April, Wang went to Hankow to discuss the proposal with party leaders.[13]

While Wang was in Hankow, however, members of the moderate and right-wing factions joined the Elder Statesmen at an April meeting in which they decided to establish a new Central Executive Committee and a new government in Nanking. The Wuhan members did not attend the meeting. Justifying the action, Ts'ai claimed that the Hankow faction had become dominated by the Communists, and that the moderates had sent a telegram to Wang and waited a week before convening the conference. To remove the Communist elements from the party, a purification campaign [Ch'ing-tang yün-tung] was planned.[14] The purge of thousands of Communists took place in Shanghai on 12 April, and the middle class rushed to support Chiang and the moderates against the radical wing in Hankow. The adherence of Ts'ai and the other Elder Statesmen to Chiang's faction brought many intellectuals into the fold.[15] A circular cablegram was issued condemning the actions of the Central Executive Committee at its third session in March and calling for a "save the party and the nation" movement [Hu-tang chiu-kuo yün-tung].[16] As a result, the government at Hankow expelled the rebel elements in Shanghai from the party.

In July, when non-Communist elements in the Wuhan government, led by Wang Ching-wei, realized the extent of the Communist plans for China, they drove the party from the Kuomintang. In August 1927, non-Communist members of the Wuhan radical wing were invited to Nanking to discuss the makeup of a new government. At the meeting, it was suggested that the Wuhan and the Nanking Executive committees be abolished and replaced by a committee, representing all factions, to organize a new government.[17] Although Wang and other members of the Wuhan faction rejected this proposal, the committee was set up.

Eventually, Wang made a further attempt to reach agreement with the moderate and right-wing factions of the party. During the fourth session of the committee, the special committee was abolished. Evidently, Ts'ai and other members opposed this move without success. The Central Executive Committee was restored to power and a government council was appointed to handle governmental affairs under the leadership of Chiang Kai-shek.[18]

During the fifth session of the Central Executive Committee, held in 1928, the Elder Statesmen tried once more to maintain the balance of power between the radical and conservative factions. Feeling that Chiang had gone too far to the left in reaching agreement with Wang's faction, they left the conference.[19] Eventually, the conference was forced to adjourn for lack of a quorum, but not before it had made several important decisions. It decided to set up a government operated by a state council and five chambers [*yüan*] under the guidance of an organic law which resembled a constitution. The Kuomintang had painfully transformed itself into the nucleus of a new government.

Ts'ai's conservative role in these confusing events has been a source of wonder to a number of his biographers. One author finds his activities incomprehensible, while a Communist source surmises that he was just "letting off a little hot air" when he approved the party purification movement.[20] Since returning to China, Ts'ai had evidently developed a strong animosity to the Communist party, a resentment which was not visible until after 1925 when he scotched the possibility of a Communist takeover in China. He himself stated that his growing hostility to the Communists resulted from their duplicity in attempting to take over the Kuomintang and from his conviction that the Communist party was a mere tool of the Soviet Union which wanted to exploit the Kuomintang as an instrument to attack the English.[21] Ts'ai also learned that Borodin had asserted "that China would have to have five million dead in order for the world revolution to succeed, and his idea was to use [China] as a sacrifice." Ts'ai's views on the Soviet Union, too, had changed radically in two years. In 1925, he had doubted that the Soviets had any interest in spreading communism in China.[22] Though detailed information about the change in Ts'ai's attitude toward communism is lacking, it seems that he was influenced by the views of his old comrades Li Shih-tseng, Chang Ching-chiang, and Wu Chih-hui, who had developed a growing hostility toward the Communist party and in the process had moved to a relatively conservative position in the Kuomintang. Chang, in particular, was close to Chiang Kai-shek. The animosity may have developed out of the split in the Work-Study Movement in France between anarchists and Communists during the 1920s.

Ts'ai and the Elder Statesmen had concluded that progress for their nation was more likely under the Kuomintang than under the Communist party. It does seem strange that he was out for blood during the party purification movement, and it is no surprise when a friend comments that Ts'ai felt uncomfortable in acceding to a policy which he did not really approve.[23] In any event, his political stance, and that of his anarchist allies, was one of mediation between the two main factions of the Kuomintang, the right-wing Western Hills group and the left wing under Wang Ching-wei, in order to form a united party and government free from Communist participation. They were influential, they backed Chiang Kai-shek, and they were ultimately successful.

Ts'ai had played a formative role in the machinations of the period and had participated in several conferences and councils set up during those years.[24] Under the new government he was appointed to the chairmanship of the Control Yuan [*Chien-ch'a-yüan*], but he felt little inclination for the censorial nature of this position. Consequently, Ts'ai assisted in the formation of the Control Yuan and then resigned, without having formally assumed office.

Problems of Education under the Republic. The years 1927 and 1928 were of transcendent importance for the future of China. They were also crucial from the point of view of educational reform. Ts'ai and other educators who had controlled educational policy under the warlord regime in Peking since the early 1920s favored a system of education which would foster the development of individualism and democracy, free from state or religious control. In "The Independence of Education," Ts'ai had voiced his hostility to political as well as religious influence in the educational system in China. "Politics," he maintained, "is the concern for immediate profit, on a short-term basis, while teaching prepares for the long-term advantage." Political parties attempt to create conformity and eliminate individuality, and are transient organizations which cannot provide a firm foundation for education.[25] Ts'ai believed that minority groups should be allowed to develop their own cultural characteristics throughout the educational system and should not have to conform to artificial patterns set by the majority group.[26] In these statements, Ts'ai seemed to contradict himself. Earlier he had said that ideas eliminated by the process of evolution, including, apparently, religious doctrine, should not be taught in public schools. How could he support minority freedom of expression with his staunch rejection of religious influence in teaching? For many minorities in China, educational freedom might well imply the right to propagate their own religious beliefs in the school system, beliefs which Ts'ai would undoubtedly label *primitive*. It seems that Ts'ai was unaware of the potential contradictions in his educational thought.

For Ts'ai, the best defense for the educational system was to guarantee its freedom from religious or political control. In "The Independence of Education," he drew on ideas which he had first broached ten years earlier as minister of education, to divide the nation into semiautonomous university districts, each with a university which would have administrative control over all elementary and secondary education within its jurisdiction. Authority within the university would be decentralized, with the chancellor chosen by an educational committee composed of the faculty. Relationships between the university districts would be managed by a committee made up of several chancellors. The Ministry of Education would have limited control and would be responsible to the chancellors, not to the central government.

Although the 1922 reform had been a step forward in terms of content, with its emphasis on democracy and internationalism, it had jurisdiction only in areas under Peking's control and was not patterned administratively after Ts'ai's anarchist ideas of decentralization. In the South, the Canton government had its own ideas about education, and in February 1926, it had created an Educational Administrative Committee to provide leadership for education at all levels.[27] By 1926, when reunification of the country under the leadership of the Kuomintang seemed possible, liberal educators began to hope that a more wide-ranging reform of education might be adopted to cover the entire nation. Since he had observed the destructive effects of the centralization of education in the early Republic, Ts'ai was eager to put his own ideas into effect. He also understood that governments and parties used education as a tool for their own benefit. Convinced that education was the blood bank of the modernization process, he desired to place it into the hands of local educators, not politicians, to make it scholastic in orientation, not bureaucratic. The French system, with its division of the nation's schools into regional areas, each responsible for the management of educational policy in its own area, was the model which appealed to him.[28]

While Ts'ai was striving to make education in China conform to his ideals, other educators were becoming critical of the Americanization of the educational system, in particular of the emphasis on internationalism and passive resistance in the new textbooks.[29] A xenophobic anti-imperialism had been on the rise in China, especially since the incident of 30 May 1925. Criticism of the "old men" who surrounded Ts'ai Yüan-p'ei and Peking University, and of their stress on humanitarianism, decentralization, and educational independence grew in Kuomintang party circles. In September 1925, the *Chung-hua Educational Review* published an article by Ch'en Ch'i-t'ien which was critical of the postwar idealism and internationalism symbolized by the 1922 reforms and called for more emphasis on patriotism and on the culture of China in the educational system. At the same time, an article in another magazine criticized Ts'ai's advisers and demanded a national system of education under strong party control.[30] Throughout party circles, there was a desire for renewed stress on Chinese history and patriotism in classrooms and in textbooks. Philosophical support for this position was frequently provided by the ideas of Fichte and Hegel, and it was maintained that nationalism was not contradictory to democracy and the development of a modern society.[31]

Despite this opposition, Ts'ai and other reformers were briefly successful in persuading the Kuomintang leadership of the feasibility of their decentralization plan, and in 1927, the Kuomintang leaders finally approved a new administrative system for education based on the regional university system in France. The country was divided into basically independent university areas, with the president of each institution responsible for the management of education in the area under his jurisdiction, thus establishing a regional rather than a centralized system of education. The new system was called the *Ta-hsüeh-yüan* ("University Council") and replaced the old Ministry of Education. Ts'ai was named chairman of the council, and because central control was limited, only three university areas [*ta-hsüeh-ch'ü*] were to be established, in Peking, Kiangsu, and Chekiang.[32]

During this period, Ts'ai returned to other educational topics which had occupied his attention in previous years. When he announced the establishment of the university council in January 1928, Ts'ai listed the three basic goals of the new system: to carry out scientific research and universalize the scientific method; to cultivate the habit of labor; and to increase interest in art.[33] His announcement indicated that the council would take specific action to forward these goals, which had been cornerstones of his earlier proposals for cultural revival as chancellor of Peking University. In order to raise the dignity of manual labor, so long despised by the literati in China, intellectuals would be encouraged to engage in physical labor whenever possible. Ts'ai also stated that he would establish a Laborer's University [*Lao-tung Ta-hsüeh*], comprising both secondary and university levels, where students would engage in physical labor as well as their studies. Night classes would be set up for rural and urban laborers. In the field of art, a music academy and art schools were also planned.

The new university council system was to be short-lived. The rising nationalist opposition, whose views conflicted sharply with those of the liberal educators, was anxious to subordinate education to political needs. For many elements in the Kuomintang, including party stalwart Ch'en Kuo-fu, students and education in general could be important instruments for expanding Kuomintang political influence and achieving social reforms in China.[34] The conflict was a concrete one; Ch'en wanted a strong, centralized educational system, under strict party control, so that education could be used as a means for propagating the party policy and destroying its enemies. Students should be encouraged to join mass organizations in order to harness their idealism for spreading the political message of the Kuomintang. For Ts'ai and the liberals, these programs were anathema. Education must be protected from government and party direction, or it could become a mere tool in political struggles. Students should devote their time entirely to education and not operate as an army of the party. China's problems required solutions that only an educated elite could provide, Ts'ai believed, and it would be wasteful to use these educational resources for agitation. Opposition came to a head at the fifth session of the Central Executive Committee, where Ching Heng-i advocated the restoration of the Educational Ministry system. The university council system was criticized for several reasons: it accented scholarship and university education at the expense of basic education at lower levels; it created several administrative problems; it was run by an irresponsible clique of educators; and it resulted in an unequal distribution of financial resources.[35]

From Ts'ai's point of view, the results of the struggle were mixed. Pressure to place education under the centralized control of government and party was too strong to resist, and within a year the government leaders abolished the university council and restored the Ministry of Education, putting education in a position where the party, not the educators, could dictate policy. Ts'ai objected to the decision, but ultimately had to acquiesce in the change. He continued to press for attention to aesthetics and advanced scholarship. As a gesture to placate the old educator, the government finally accepted one aspect of the university council system, the new academic research institute, Academia Sinica [*Chung-yang Yen-chiu-yüan*], which had been established in 1927 with Ts'ai as chairman and which was designed as a high-level institute to encourage the development of research in the natural and social sciences. Ts'ai would head the institute for the remainder of his life.

With the university council abolished and a new ministry created in late 1928, Ts'ai declined to continue his involvement with ministerial affairs and decided to concentrate on his work at the institute. The current of educational policy was running against his emphasis on scholarship and in the direction of state and party control. As a result of the changes of 1928, many of the reforms which Ts'ai had painstakingly advocated during the previous decade were dismantled. The new educational program had as its aims the realization of Sun's Three People's Principles (nationalism, democracy, and people's livelihood) and, in order to achieve national unity and a sense of identity, the utilization of traditional ethical concepts such as filial piety, loyalty, sincerity, and righteousness. In the new program, religion was regulated, and textbooks were to stress nationalism, the spirit of protest, political consciousness, anti-imperialism, and social freedom, rather than individualist democracy.[36]

On one issue, however, Ts'ai's views were ultimately victorious. Communist activity in the student movement was increasing, and the Kuomintang leadership, which was concerned over Communist infiltration of student organizations, began to discourage student activism and interference in politics. From Ts'ai's point of view, however, students were encouraged to concentrate on their studies for the wrong reason. The new trend in education, he believed, was a defeat of the ideas he had propagated for so many years, a rejection of humanitarianism, individualism, and educational independence.

Despite his failure, Ts'ai continued to speak out on educational matters during the last decade of his life. Social and economic problems had not disappeared with the establishment of the Nanking government and could no longer be blamed on warlord misrule. The government took Sun Yat-sen's program as its guide for modernization and declared China to be in Sun's second stage, the period of political tutelage, when society would be cured of its ignorance and prepared for democracy. For Ts'ai, education was the key to the problem. He still participated in many educational conferences that convened during the 1930s, and one of his main concerns was the problem of universal education. This was one of the most important facets of the tutelage period, and a program for realizing obligatory education had been on the books for several years, but without notable success. Financial resources, teachers, and schools were not available in sufficient quantities, and in the early 1930s, only slightly over 21 percent of all school-age children were in school.[37]

Realizing that the established method of tying universal education with elementary education had failed, Ts'ai stated that the program of enforcing a four-year compulsory program at the elementary level was beyond China's present resources and suggested that older children (ten to eleven years of age) who had been deprived of elementary education be given a brief compulsory educational program. Although the period of compulsory schooling would be shortened from earlier suggestions, it would be more strictly enforced. Ts'ai's suggestion was accepted, and in 1935, children aged ten to sixteen were required to attend a short-term elementary school for at least one year. At the same time, the government enforced compulsory attendance in schools on a nation-wide basis.[38]

Mass education was not the only problem affecting the educational system during the 1930s. Unemployment, a condition stemming partly from the worldwide depression, had struck China with some force, and many were saying that obligatory education would only add to the unemployment problem. In 1932, Ch'en Kuo-fu suggested that schools give less attention to subjects such as law, literature, and art, and more to vocational education in order to maximize the opportunities for employment after a student has left school. Ch'en's suggestion met with agreement in Chinese educational circles, as well as among the members of an International Committee on Chinese Education under the direction of the League of Nations. After 1933, the government tried to discourage high-level students from entering the humanities and to persuade them to enter practical fields.[39]

The attacks on the humanities posed a problem for Ts'ai Yüan-p'ei. Although he recognized the need in China for an increase in vocational education, he also believed in the benefits of a humanist form of education, and it is probable that he only reluctantly helped sponsor the new emphasis on practical education. He conceded publicly that the nation could not afford to train an intellectual elite in pure scholarship during the period of political tutelage.[40] Perhaps he was able to console himself that the new emphasis on vocational education to encourage Chinese productive capacity was in line with his desire to raise the dignity of manual labor and nourish a higher level of scientific and technological knowledge in the population. Nevertheless, he did see vocational education as an opportunity for China to cure one of its traditional bad habits, a tendency to downgrade technological expertise.[41]

Student activism was another aspect of education that caused concern during the early 1930s. Although Ts'ai had called for educational reform throughout his mature life, he was now ceasing to symbolize student demands in the way he had done during the new culture period. Since his return from Europe in 1926, he had counseled students to concentrate on their studies, not on political activities. Student involvement and concern over world and national affairs had not declined, however, and culminated in riots over the loss of Manchuria to Japan in September 1931. The distance from 1919 was underscored on 15 December, when radical students, demonstrating against the government's inability to resist Japan, broke into central party headquarters in Peiping and mauled Ts'ai and Ch'en Ming-shu, who had just left a party committee meeting.[42] Ts'ai responded calmly to the incident, finding it symbolic of the failure of his own generation to solve the nation's problems. He also felt that the incident had been inspired by extremist elements and did not represent the feelings of the average student:

> If only the youthful patriotic movement took the form of instructing illiterates during vacation, or sending telegrams to express their opinions, then we could agree that its effects were wholly beneficial. But the student patriotic movement these days emphasizes striking from classes and demonstrating. . . . Such methods are only a sacrifice of time and education.[43]

The root of China's problem, he declared, lies in its weakness in science, and only through study can this weakness be resolved. Just think, he added wistfully, how many potential Krupps, Pasteurs, and Edisons there are who should be in class studying, not out in the streets demonstrating.

Problems of Democracy During the Period of Political Tutelage. Ts'ai and the other Elder Statesmen had gambled that a Kuomintang government under Chiang Kai-shek, while not ideal from their theoretical point of view, would be better than any of the realistic alternatives offered during the 1920s. Application of Sun's directives for carrying out the Three People's Principles and attention given to the broadening of democratic values during the tutelage period of the revolution would, in their eyes, do more to further the realization of anarchist ideals than any previous government had done. The long controversy over educational reform in the late 1920s soured Ts'ai to some extent, however, on the direction the new government was going to take. It also symbolized the gap between Ts'ai's ideas and those of the government and party leadership. Younger men with a different perspective on life and the needs of society were rising to the top of the Kuomintang power structure; consequently, the liberal humanism and internationalism of Ts'ai's prime, which appealed to a large minority of party members in earlier years, seemed to find little reflection in high places in society. In the thirties, Ts'ai occasionally made political headlines, but his role in national politics was definitely fading. He gradually divested himself of all active participation in government and party councils and concentrated his energies on his work at the institute.[44] This eclipse during the thirties is understandable. He had always been more a theorist than an implementer of policy, stronger on establishing principles than on carrying out already determined policy. And this was not a time for theory and principle, but for the practical application of the theories of Sun Yat-sen to republican China. The libertarian ideals of the survivors of the new culture period were not welcome in the new atmosphere.

When Ts'ai participated in government and party affairs during the last years of his life, he advocated the policies laid down by his Kuomintang colleague Sun Yat-sen and sometimes played Sun's old role of party mediator, much as he had in the years of the early Republic. During the intraparty squabbles which occurred during the Nanking period, Ts'ai continued to hold a balance between radicals and conservatives, and often stepped in to maintain party harmony.[45] Although he was still an active party man, he appeared to be unhappy over the trend of events in China. He was particularly concerned about the strength of the Communist party which, he felt, exercised "an almost religious fascination" over much of the rural population. Unless it could be eliminated, it would be like giving wings to a tiger, "begetting endless sorrow." He did not doubt the ability of the Nationalist government to "clip the wings of the fierce tiger," but the nature of the government's counterattack concerned him. If the government did not develop a "positive program," he felt, and if it "return[ed] to the old greedy officials, the local rascals and oppressive gentry, that would be an encouragement to the red bandits to recover their lost ground."[46] If discontent in the rural areas increased, it could only redound to the benefit of the Communists and their theory of class struggle. Evidently, Ts'ai had marked up his estimate of the potential strength of the Communists in China.

To eradicate the poison of Communism and restore confidence in the government in Nanking, Ts'ai recommended a strict adherence to the local government program advocated by Sun Yat-sen for the tutelage period: to improve local social and economic conditions, to build schools, and to construct the foundation of local democracy. Ts'ai worried that these policies were not being followed in areas under Nanking's control, and he took the government to task for its negligence.

Yet Ts'ai's hostility to the Communist party is misleading, for in reality he seemed to be moving toward the left during the last years of his life. He had not lost his interest in socialism or in the doctrines of Karl Marx as a result of his dislike of the local Communist movement. In a preface to *A History of Socialism,* written in 1920, Ts'ai had discussed the antecedents of socialism in China and made favorable comments on its development in Europe. At that time, however, he showed more interest in syndicalism, which flourished among anarchists in the West after World War I, and he suggested that the Chinese labor movement look into the possibilities of syndicalist theory.[47] Ts'ai's interest in Marx continued into the thirties, despite his hostility to Communist activities in China. In a preface to Li Chi's *Biography of Marx,* he lamented that as a result of the conflict between the government and the Communist party, people were afraid to discuss the Soviet Union or even Karl Marx, whom Ts'ai called a great modern philosopher. In 1933, in a volume commemorating the fiftieth anniversary of Marx's death, he said that it was necessary to distinguish between Marxism and the Chinese Communist party. Ts'ai advocated an expansion of Marxist studies in China, in accordance with practice where translations of Marx's writings were readily available.[48] Obviously, Ts'ai was unhappy about the restrictions on freedom of speech in republican China and called the government's censorship policy "intellectual Boxerism." The government must have been equally disturbed at Ts'ai's criticism, but because of his prominence and increasing age, they left him alone.

Ts'ai's reaction to government censorship during the 1930s was only one facet of his reaction to the authoritarianism of the Nanking regime. The National government, concerned over its inability to root out Communist influence in China, engaged in a severe repression of persons and groups considered subversive to Kuomintang policies. Liberals began to voice criticism of government security methods, contending that persons arrested for political reasons were being detained without charge in Chinese prisons. Ts'ai, a defender of the individual against the tyranny of the majority, invested his own reputation in the movement to guarantee individual rights and freedom of speech. In June 1932, he complained about the arrest of two alleged foreign spies, a husband and wife by the name of Noulens, who were suspected of Communist conspiracy and held without trial for thirteen months.[49] In December, angered over the arrest of Ch'en Tu-hsiu, still a Communist but expelled from the party in 1932, and now a leader of a Trotskyite faction, Ts'ai helped to establish the Chinese League for the Protection of Civil Rights [*Chung-kuo Min-ch'uan Pao-chang T'ung-meng*]. The league was formed to protect individuals imprisoned by the government, mostly members of the left wing, from arbitrary punishment.[50] The league may have been inspired by the Communist party, although little is known about its origins. However, it attracted support from well-known intellectuals not directly connected with the Communist movement in China, including Lu Hsün, Hu Shih, Lin Yu-t'ang, Yang Ch'uan (Ts'ai's young assistant at the Academia Sinica), Ch'en Pin-ho, and Yi Lo-sheng.[51] Ts'ai was one of the most prominent members of the league, and on 30 December, he convened a press conference in which he stated his reasons for joining the organization. The League, he said, was designed to represent no particular party or faction, but would protect the rights of all mankind. His primary concern was the rights of citizens against arbitrary arrest and punishment. There was "no difference in rights," he said, "between a man not yet convicted and one already convicted. A man not yet tried and convicted should not be subject to arbitrary behavior. But a man already convicted should also have his natural rights preserved, because it is always possible that there has been an injustice."[52] Criminologists, Ts'ai continued, are finding that the crimes committed by men are often the result of their environment. Socialists claim that behavior stems from class background. Men should not, in any case, be punished without due process of law.

During a 6 February 1933 meeting of the league, chaired by Ts'ai, resolutions were passed urging that the national emergency criminal code be abolished and that all punishments not in accordance with normal legal procedures be abandoned. The government, however, was not long in reacting to the league. It criticized members of the organization for "foolishly defending" Communists and counterrevolutionaries, thereby doing harm to the credibility of their group.[53] Demands began to be heard that the league should be abolished, and moderates such as Hu Shih withdrew. When Yang Ch'uan, the secretary of the league, was mysteriously assassinated, the government suspended the activities of the organization.

Ts'ai's participation in the league was not an isolated incident and indicates that his anarchist heart was increasingly disturbed at the lack of freedom in China. Besides showing an open interest in Marxist studies in China, Ts'ai displeased the government in October 1936 when he joined Soong Ch'ing-ling and others in settling the funeral affairs of Lu Hsün, the leftist writer who had become persona non grata with the government. If Ts'ai was aware of the radical nature of these groups, and of their likely connection with the Communist party, it did not prevent him from joining in their activities.

In Quest of the Golden Mean. The internal struggle over Westernization, which had been a major issue on the intellectual scene even before 1900, had not been resolved by the New Culture Movement and its stormy aftermath. During the new culture period, the argument over Westernization had raged between two virtually opposite poles—advocates of Westernization such as Ch'en Tu-hsiu and Hu Shih versus defenders of the traditional order such as Ku Hung-ming, Lin Shu, and Liu Shih-p'ei. Admittedly, there were those who viewed reform as a process of gradual synthesis, from the tradition-minded Liang Ch'i-ch'ao to the reform-minded Ts'ai Yüan-p'ei. Even Hu Shih had admitted on a theoretical basis that some useful aspects of traditional culture should be maintained, although suitably styled for modern consumption. In general, the stress in the reform movement during the early Republic had been one of comprehensive Westernization, from its political and social institutions to the way China should dress, eat, and think.

In the postwar years, the traditional culture enjoyed a modest revival, even among some advocates of moderate reform. There is a wide variety of reasons for this, although it seems generally true that the revival was caused not by a greater confidence in the traditional order, but by a decreasing trust in Western panaceas. In part, it was a reaction to events in the West—the war, the postwar depression, and the growing *Weltschmerz* of European intellectuals (which had a striking effect on Chinese travelers such as Liang Chi'i-ch'ao and Carson Chang); resentment at Western behavior toward China, from the Versailles decision to the Western recognition of the legitimacy of the government in Peking; and fear of rising radicalism in China as evidenced by the founding of the Communist party. The change was bound to come following the idealism about Western culture that existed during the first decade of the Republic.

Ts'ai, like many other Chinese of the day, was affected by World War I and postwar events in China and Europe. In early days, he had seemed to be an unrestrained admirer of the West. Although he had implied that cultural interchange was a two-way street, he had never been clear about the contribution China herself could make. Western culture, with its democratic institutions and material prosperity, had seemed an almost unblemished vision of progress, from a material as well as a spiritual point of view. China, by comparison, had to make up for lost ground. Only in the distant future would China revitalize her creative energies and do her part to enrich the human experience. For the moment, he seemed to say, China would be content to borrow, not to lend.

At the end of the war, Ts'ai was still calling the allied victory a symbol of the success of Mutual Aid in the world. At the same time, he also conceded that Europe was not the paragon of success that she had seemed, and that China would yet play an active role in the progress of mankind. Cultural interchange would be, after all, a two-way process. This is a familiar attitude, reminiscent of the gleeful reaction of Liang and Yen Fu to the agony of Europe and might indicate that Ts'ai, after all, was looking for a way to salvage national and cultural pride, to show that China, too, had much to offer.

It is difficult, at this distance, to determine what went on in the old educator's mind. But I think that other concerns dictated Ts'ai's partial change of heart. The fact is, he was becoming aware of Western weaknesses—economic inequality, capitalism, and militarism. Like traditionalists and Marxists, he was ready to concede that European society did not embody the perfection that it had once seemed to possess. He even agreed with the traditionalists who stated that the West needed some of the solid old virtues of the East to make up for its deficiencies. In effect, Ts'ai echoed the familiar theme that the "materialist" West needed the "spirituality" of China. It is doubtful, however, that he was motivated solely by a need to justify China in her own eyes, to damn Europe in order to praise China; his primary concern was the preservation of the fragile roots of science and democracy that he had carefully nurtured through the early republican period. World War I, he emphasized, did not disclose the bankruptcy of science, as maintained by Liang and Carson Chang, or of liberal democracy, as maintained by the Marxists. Science and democracy continued to be the best hope for China and for humanity as a whole. Nevertheless, the war demonstrated that the West occasionally stumbled on the road to utopia. China should not abandon the road to democracy and science, but she should look to her own resources to make up the Western deficiency—and even offer the West a helping hand in its own time of stress.

Ts'ai had begun elaborating on these views long before 1919 gave rise to anti-Westernism, which was always under the surface in China. He broached this point of view even while on other occasions he was extolling the Great War as the triumph of Mutual Aid over the powers of darkness in human society. In an address before the Chinese Social and Political Science Association in 1918, Ts'ai contrasted Eastern and Western society, mentioning a number of areas in which China could make a positive contribution to world progress.[54] He tried to explain how a society so advanced in scientific achievement and individual freedom could descend to the self-destruction of the war. In the process, he mentioned aspects of Western civilization to which he had never alluded in the first years of the Republic.

Ts'ai's point of view presaged many of the criticisms which would soon be leveled at Western civilization by Bertrand Russell and the

97

Chinese neo-traditionalists.[55] He was critical of the very qualities of energetic self-assertion that Yen Fu had found engaging twenty years before. The modern West, he contended, tends to go to extremes. It was too aggressive, too prone to emphasize material qualities, too legalistic, and too little inclined to appreciate humanistic values. Ts'ai did not claim that China possessed virtues where the West had only flaws. On the contrary, China's problem in each case was the tendency to the opposite extreme, to be passive and accept stagnation as a permanent quality of life, to be pacifistic, and to be slipshod in establishing laws to govern human society.

He was sensitive to the weaknesses in both civilizations, and was searching for a Golden Mean which could incorporate the virtues and avoid the insufficiencies of each culture. The answer, he maintained, lay not at the two extremes, but in a compromise of the antithetical extremes achieved through cultural interchange. The West could lead China to a greater reliance on law, while China could persuade the West to place greater trust in personal virtue in order to achieve compliance with the standards of society. Indicating that the two cultures were moving closer together in this respect, he asserted that Herbert Spencer's individualistic philosophy and the growing popularity of coalition cabinets in the European nations showed "a departure from the rule of law and more stress . . . upon the personal element."[56] China, on the other hand, was adopting the Western concepts of constitutional government and the rule of law.

A middle road had to be found between Western aggressiveness and Chinese passivity. China's emphasis on harmony and tranquillity had arrested the development of her scientific and artistic creativity. The Western emphasis on constant expansion, on the other hand, had its corresponding drawback, the utter despair common in the West to those left behind in the struggle for existence. Where Spencer and Yen Fu had seen individual failure as a regrettable but necessary concomitant of progress, Ts'ai hoped to find a middle way. China, he said, was developing her industrial capacity, while the West was learning to appreciate the pacifist doctrine of Leo Tolstoi.

In essence, Ts'ai believed that the progress of humanity could be realized through a moderation of the extreme tendencies found in East and West. China and the West should recognize their own flaws and learn to conquer them through greater familiarity with each other. Ts'ai's sensitivity to modern problems is revealed in this article. In other ways, it shows him at his weakest. He pretends to maintain that familiarity, or cultural interchange, leads to the resolution of cultural flaws, yet in few of his examples is there any attempt to prove that the West had indeed been influenced by the Chinese example. Even if his examples drawn from both societies were valid, they did no more than indicate a gradual moderation of the extreme tendencies in the two cultures, not that this process was a result of cultural interchange. More disconcerting, however, was his choice of examples, which showed little perspicacity in the understanding of history. The article is revealing, however, in showing his private reaction to the European war. Where publicly Ts'ai had felt obliged to defend the war as a victory over evil, in a more reflective moment he revealed his new doubts about the quality of contemporary European civilization.

Ts'ai continued to develop these ideas in speeches and articles during the next few years. His main theme was the point he had made earlier, that China's traditional penchant for moderation, her emphasis on harmony, tolerance, and humanism, all original Confucian qualities, would be a useful antidote to the materialistic and aggressive tendencies of Western society. But where in 1918 he had implied that the ideal human qualities lay in a compromise between Chinese and Western culture, he now asserted that the very quality of moderation that was necessary to attain the final utopia could be found in traditional Chinese humanism. Moreover, he found in traditional China other qualities that were useful in the modern day: democracy (through Mencius, the Mandate of Heaven, and the civil service examination system), internationalism (the Confucian rejection of narrow nationalism), and equality (the ancient well-field system and the clan system, which obliged the rich to share with the poor). Moderation, though, was the greatest quality of the Chinese people. And China's traditional equability could be a valuable gift to humanity, for it was not common in the Western world where extreme solutions such as Nietzsche's individualism and Tolstoi's extreme pacifism proliferated. The last great exponent of moderation in Europe, he maintained, was Aristotle, whose Doctrine of the Golden Mean resembled the Confucian Doctrine of the Mean. China, on the other hand, traditionally rejected extremist theories, such as legalism and Taoism, and cultivated the moderation of Confucius. This tendency to compromise and assimilate would soften the brutal conflicts of this transitional age.

In later years, Ts'ai occasionally attempted to weave Sun Yat-sen's Three Peoples' Principles into China's penchant for moderation. In a speech before the Royal Asiatic Society in November 1930, he sounded almost like a party hack in his praise of Sun's philosophy. Sun's thought, he maintained, was a contemporary manifestation of China's belief in the Golden Mean.[57] Some nationalists in China opposed the principle of *Ta-t'ung* as an element which was detrimental to patriotic spirit, while many Chinese internationalists opposed nationalism as an offense to the spirit of international harmony. Sun's principle of nationalism, he claimed, is aimed at developing China's patriotic spirit and attaining true political independence. At the same time, however, it emphasizes the political and racial equality of all races and nationalities. Other examples of Sun's moderation were his avoidance of totalitarianism and anarchy (he gave the government the capacity to rule, while permitting the people to participate in the governing process) and his concepts of land equalization and regulation of capital, which avoid the extremes of capitalism and Marxist communism. Sun had absorbed the values of the West, its talent for political organization and scientific development, and then modified them through China's ability to take the middle road. This was the greatness of his program. Through Sun's philosophy, China could avoid the severities of the political and economic revolutions occurring in Europe.[58]

Ts'ai's shift in attitude, on the surface, almost seems to be an elaboration of the old statement that the East is "spirit" and the West is "material." There is no doubt that the war had affected his attitude toward Western civilization and made him more wary of its value to China. It also led him into a nostalgic appreciation of the old virtues of Confucian civilization, virtues which he hardly thought about during his revolutionary days in Shanghai. But Ts'ai's new reliance on Confucian humanism should not be seen as a triumphant reaffirmation of Chinese culture in the face of the Western onslaught. As before, Ts'ai was trying to preserve the democratic and humanist aspects of China's cultural revival. If the West could not provide them, then China would have to call on the humanist side of her own tradition to make up the deficiency. In a sense, this is the old spirit-matter argument restated; and perhaps Ts'ai exaggerated the old virtues. It is not likely, however, that he felt a great sense of cultural satisfaction in doing so. Rather, Ts'ai must have felt a sense of loss at the failure of the West to live up to his hopes. China's disillusion with Western democracy in the 1920s, the root of so many of his problems, must have been a bitter blow to Ts'ai and probably forced him to readjust his estimate of the immanence of the Ta-t'ung. He must have turned to Confucious with mixed emotions.

Evidently, the new government leadership established in Nanking after 1927 was not plagued with doubts and indecision about such questions. Sun Yat-sen had left an ideological legacy which attempted to maintain a balance between reform and tradition, but with an emphasis on change. Under his successor Chiang Kai-shek, a man with perhaps a certain distrust of intellectuals and liberal ideas, China began to return to a more traditional stance.[59] Chiang advocated a blend of East and West reminiscent of Chang Chih-tung's old recipe. Distrustful of Western liberalism as well as of communism, Chiang prescribed for China a synthetic ideology based on a combination of Western science and traditional social philosophy. Western technology would be used to strengthen the nation, but Western individualism and the liberal concept of a limitation on state power was explicitly rejected as foreign

*

100

to Chinese experience and Chinese needs. The inapplicability of many of the old political and social institutions was conceded, but the Confucian ethical essence was triumphantly reasserted, if with an air of defensive pride. The Chiang Kai-shek government was not bashful about putting the new formula into practice. Schools were informed that a greater emphasis on the Confucian classics was expected. A New Life Movement [*Hsin sheng-huo yün-tung*] was even established to inculcate neo-Confucianism into the body politic.

There were intellectual offshoots of this new trend, and the long controversy over Westernization reached a new climax in 1935, when a group of ten professors published a demand for the construction of a Chinese standard culture [*Chung-kuo Pen-wei Wen-hua*]. If there comes a time in any controversy when all the arguments have been set forth, and when the contestants are reduced to a mere repetition of points long since established, then, with the 1935 statement and its ensuing controversy, such a time had been reached in the old East-West argument. It was a rehash of old arguments, with each side sparring more with a sterile ghost from the past than with the real issues. The professors argued that China should construct a standard culture for herself, if she wished to retain her "unique political, social and intellectual qualities" and maintain "a certain degree of cultural influence" in the world.[60] They stated that such a culture had to be established on the basis of a synthesis of values from East and West, and such values could be constructed only on the basis of critical empirical analysis. China must borrow in order to survive, they said, and they rejected the ideas of those "who maintain that China should return to the past; ancient China has already become history, and history cannot, and need not, flourish again." On the other hand, China should not attempt to imitate the West blindly: "There are those who think that China should entirely imitate the Anglo-Saxon nations; England and America have their own special characteristics, of course, but China, which is not England or America, should have her own unique conscious form." Therefore, blatant imitation of Anglo-Saxon liberalism, German national socialism, or Russian communism is unwise, since none of these systems could be suitable to China's "special character." China, they said, is contemporary China and not ancient China, and it should have its own modern character. They concluded that "the past should be examined, and what should be maintained can continue to exist, while the irrelevant can be discarded. . . . As for Western culture, let us absorb what is of value only. . . . In building this China, we are not abandoning the ideal of the *Ta-t'ung,* but are first constructing China, and then she can assist in the struggle for the *Ta-t'ung.*"

If the statement had been issued in a cultural and historical vacuum, it would have been innocuous. Certainly, Westernizers such as Hu Shih had expressed themselves in similar terms over the years, and Ts'ai had long advocated such a broad synthetic approach. On the face of it, therefore, the professorial statement was an attempt to formulate a middle position between total Westernization, without consideration for the special characteristics of the Chinese, and a mossback traditionalism, which denied any validity to Western institutions in China. The statement, however, was not given in a cultural vacuum, and it evoked in the reader memories of all that had been said in China on the subject for the last half century, from Chang Chih-tung's "essence versus practical use" dichotomy through Liang Sou-ming's "East is spirit and West is material" down to the present. To a Westernizer, the statement was but a smoke screen for the advocates of neo-traditionalism to bring in the old rotten culture. In an acid reply to the statement, Hu Shih snapped that the professors were just voicing a modern version of Chang Chih-tung's self-strengthening thesis, with the *pen-wei* ("the standard") as the old *t'i*. He conceded that the professors themselves might have been unconscious of the implications of their position, but he maintained that the argument allowed all reactionaries in China to defend whatever they considered to be essential.[61] The most diehard reactionary would not object to riding in Western automobiles, he said, and any stubborn conservative would not be uncomfortable under the professors' banner.

Perhaps Hu was being unfair to the professors. He was responding to criticism which had been obviously directed at him, and he could with justification be accused of exaggeration. The professors did not deny the value of the "spiritual" side of Western civilization, and they made no specific reference to areas in which Chinese culture was superior to that of the West. But there were problems connected with their hypothesis, and they were quickly attacked by critics who wanted to know more specifically what the professors had in mind. What did they mean by a "standard culture"? On what basis could value be determined? Was not the whole idea of scientific analysis meaningless, since value is always subjective?[62] In the controversy, which excited moderate attention in some scholarly and semischolarly journals for a few weeks, the professors were on the defensive and were not very clear about their standard of value. One asserted, as an example, that China had no need to adopt Western institutions such as Christianity and capitalism, but made no attempt to justify his argument by empirical means.

Although the arguments as a rule are sterile, they reflect some differences, mainly between those who felt that China had to adopt all of the West in order to make a successful modernization and those who felt that a selective approach was preferable. Much of this hairsplitting illustrated that China had not come very far in nearly fifty years in determining on what basis China should adopt foreign values. There was still a general agreement that some form of synthesis of East and West was the best policy, but China's leaders recognized that Western values could not be selected aimlessly, like goods on a shelf. For the Westernizer, to obtain Western democracy, it was also necessary to adopt Western methods of production. But, as the professors had pointed out, no society can take on foreign values without reference to its own heritage. China was obviously in a dilemma, and the professors had attempted to find a way out.

Ts'ai became indirectly involved in the "standard culture" controversy. Superficially, the statement resembles his own views, but he also took issue with the professorial position. Like Hu Shih, Ts'ai sensed that the position permitted conservatives to pose obstacles to needed reforms in order to hold on to some of the bones and seeds of the old culture. In a reply to Ho Ping-sung, one of the signatories of the professorial statement, Ts'ai said that it was empty talk to discuss what was the national heritage of China. China, he said, should undertake a scientific analysis of values from all cultures, adopting only what is of value to her. Then she can look back to see what has remained of the traditional heritage.[63] Ts'ai, in other words, wanted to change the emphasis: not to study what was of value in the Chinese heritage, and then borrow what was needed, but to concentrate on the determination of value, regardless of national origin. Significantly, however, Ts'ai did not reject the selective approach entirely, but wanted to begin with an emphasis on *value,* not on preserving China's *essence* in a standard culture.[64] Ts'ai did not add much clarity to the controversy. He failed to address himself to either of the basic premises of the opposing sides —the insistence of the Westernizers that values cannot be selected at random, and the argument of traditionalists that each society must preserve its cultural essence. At most, he had added another dimension to an already confused situation.

After 1935, Ts'ai began to take less interest in national affairs, having been seriously hampered by illness. He had been concerned over Japanese aggression in North China, and on one occasion expressed a desire to go abroad to build up foreign sympathy with China. Meeting Wang Ching-wei on a train when Wang was becoming friendly with Japan, Ts'ai asked him to support resistance against the aggressors from the north. A friend recollected that he told Wang, "We ought to be firm about the Sino-Japanese situation, and should resist with all our hearts. Only if we resist will the next generation be able to resist, and will China be able to find a way out."[65]

When Shanghai fell to the Japanese, Ts'ai had to give up his residence in China and move to Hong Kong. He had already resigned most of his activities and hoped to devote his remaining years to scholarship. At one time, he expressed a desire to follow the National government to its mountain retreat in Chungking, but his health was failing and he was unable to leave the British colony. In Hong King, he seldom made a public appearance. Friends reported that he was still reading philosophy and could frequently be seen on a simple rattan chair in his patio, reading ten lines at a glance. A serious illness finally took his life on 5 March 1940, at the age of seventy-two. A good friend, Chou Hsin, was at his side when the end came. According to Chou, Ts'ai's last intelligible words were "Science and aesthetics can save the nation."[66] At the last, he had not altered his testament to China.

8

Conclusion

In the broadest sense, it might be said that there are two major strains in the social and cultural Chinese revolution of the twentieth century—the drive for national revival and the humanist urge to build a new democratic and egalitarian society. To a degree, these urges are complementary, and it is likely that all progressive Chinese, from Liang Ch'i-ch'ao to Mao Tse-tung, have been motivated by both strains. It is also clear that different individuals placed different priorities on the attainment of these goals, and that there have been major differences within the progressive movement over the methods of attaining them.

Within this broad spectrum of opinion and action, Ts'ai Yüan-p'ei falls within the humanist strain of the Chinese Cultural Revolution. Although he understood the problem of national survival and its relationship to the nation-building effort, he was more concerned with the quality of the lives of the individuals in society and with the fate of mankind as a whole.

As we have seen, the sources of Ts'ai's humanistic thought are varied —in the Western liberal democratic tradition, in the anarchist offshoot of Western utopianism, in the ethical and metaphysical ideas of German Neo-Kantianism, and, not least, in the humanistic elements in the Confucian heritage itself. It would perhaps be impossible to trace Ts'ai's ideas to a single source, for it is apparent that he was highly eclectic in his approach and selected those elements which he found useful in fashioning a coherent philosophy of life and a program for social change. In the process, he changed all that he touched and eventually formulated a program and an ideology for the new China that was unique in its totality, if not in each of its elements.

In the final analysis, it might be said that the taproot of Ts'ai's world view was a modernized version of the humanistic Confucian tradition. It was in his youth, as a student in a strongly traditional society, that he first betrayed the ethical and even puritanical strain in his thought. It was here, indeed, that his belief in an essentially moral, but impersonal universe, in the reliance on ethics rather than on government regulation and law to obtain compliance with the needs of the community, in the dual emphasis on self-cultivation and service to society, was inculcated into his character. In some respects, he would depart from traditional Confucian doctrine in later years, but it might be maintained that he had woven Western concepts into a familiar Confucian fabric. This Confucian cast to his thought had led many of his contemporaries to see him, in retrospect, almost entirely in Confucian terms, as a Confucian mandarin in Western dress. Certainly, in his personal demeanor he reflected the age-old image of the Confucian gentleman.

Eventually, Confucianism became too restrictive, and by the turn of the century, Ts'ai had begun to supplement it with new ideas from abroad. But it is clear that he selected those elements which did the least violence to his Confucian humanist leanings. He turned to Kropotkin's Mutual Aid rather than social Darwinism, to Kant rather than philosophical materialism, to Western liberal democracy rather than the statism of Japan and Germany. Thus Ts'ai's response to Western thought was shaped as much by Confucian tradition as any of his well-known contemporaries.

In effect, Ts'ai had used the evidence of Western experience to bolster the assumptions that he had developed out of his own educational experience as a youth. While Yen Fu and Liang Ch'i-ch'ao had chosen social Darwinism as a pseudo-scientific crutch for their own social and political theories, Ts'ai turned to the variegated world of Western thought to supplement the Confucian humanist tendencies that had already characterized his thought in his youth.

Despite Ts'ai's efforts, the humanist side of the Chinese Cultural Revolution is not strongly reflected today on the Chinese mainland or on the island of Taiwan. Although neither government rejects democracy as an expression of the ideal, they both tend to stress the nation at the expense of the individual, contending that in perilous times the needs of society are foremost. During the course of the Chinese Revolution, those who attempted to raise the quality of individual lives and not just the power of the state were running against the grain of history.

We may regret that the humanist rose failed to flower in modern China, and it is easy to blame those who have taken China along a different road. Yet, from our vantage point in history, it is evident that the humanist vision, after a brief hope of success in the early Republic, had little relevance in the world of political struggle, hatred, ignorance, and poverty that characterized early twentieth-century China. In the conditions of the time, men would not assume that their opponents were good and honorable men. Nor could the masses free themselves from the shackles of their environment without strong leadership.

In effect, Ts'ai and his humanist allies had seen what may yet be a vision of China's future, but they had badly misinterpreted the needs of the time. Liberalism and anarchism had risen in the West against the evils of statism and big government, institutional obstacles to human freedom and happiness. In republican China, the problem was not too much government power, but too little. What was needed was a reform-minded elite to lift the nation out of its lethargy and construct a new society.

To most of his contemporaries, therefore, Ts'ai's program did not answer the real problems of modern China. Humanism was seen as a luxury the nation could not afford. Ts'ai refused to concede this premise and insisted on the need for humanism to the end of his life. In the twilight of his career, he did admit that it was no time for optimism. In an interview with a reporter from *Time* magazine, Ts'ai complained that the contemporary world had come to worship materialism.[1] Materialism had caused World War I, and a second conflict was on the horizon. Man created the machine, and now he was a slave to it, and an enemy to his own kind. What he said was not unique, but it was significant coming from one of China's great optimists and advocates of science, a sad acknowledgement of what he had feared two decades earlier. Still, Ts'ai did not deny science its role. The solution was not to abandon science, but to develop aesthetics. Although it was not a total solution, it might at least cut off the ominous sprouts of a new war. But Ts'ai had few illusions, and his tone was that of a disappointed man.

From today's perspective, the humanist strain seems like a memory from the distant past, an expression of human optimism unlikely to provide a realistic basis for Chinese policy in the foreseeable future. Was the humanistic strain, then, without any but historical significance, a castle of sand destined to be washed away by the incoming tide of social revolution?

Perhaps a tentative comparison with the Renaissance and the rise of modern Europe is not out of place. It is worthwhile to recall that early modern Europe was a time of rising nationalism, of frequent internal strife, and of violent social change. At the same time, however, it witnessed the growth of a secular humanism, a new concern for the ultimate oneness and worth of all men. In the long run, humanism survived and became the foundation of the rise of liberal democracy in many societies in Western civilization. There are perhaps few grounds for belief that China will follow the historical pattern of the modern West. On the other hand, it is not impossible that out of these times of tension and turmoil will come a new Chinese society which will reflect China's quest for human dignity and brotherhood.

In that sense, Ts'ai may not have had his last word. So long as the humanist vision is seen as a worthwhile ideal—and there are signs of this trend in the recent Great Proletarian Cultural Revolution—it is not hopelessly out of reach. And if China looks on humanism as an attainable goal, it may yet be realized. In these days, only idealists like Ts'ai Yüan-p'ei can have the confidence that China, and mankind itself, can attain such a Golden Age.

Notes

Sources in Chinese most frequently cited in the text, including abbreviations used in the notes, are listed below. Details on other sources utilized in the preparation of this study can be found in the notes.

CC   *Ts'ai Yüan-p'ei hsien-sheng ch'uan-chi* [The Complete Works of Mr. Ts'ai Yüan-p'ei]. Taipei: Commercial Press, 1968.

HC   *Ts'ai Yüan-p'ei hsuan-chi* [A Selection of the Writings of Ts'ai Yüan-p'ei]. Taipei: Book World, 1963.

IWLC   Sun Te-chung, ed. *Ts'ai Yüan-p'ei hsien-sheng i-wen lei-ch'ao* [A Selection of the Posthumous Writings of Mr. Ts'ai Yüan-p'ei]. Taipei: Fu-hsing Shu-chü, 1961.

Chapter 1

1. Hao Chang, *Liang Ch'i-ch'ao and Intellectual Transition in China, 1890–1907* (Cambridge: Harvard University Press, 1971), p. 2.

2. Benjamin Schwartz, "Some Polarities in Confucian Thought," in David S. Nivison, ed., *Confucianism in Action* (Stanford: Stanford University Press, 1959), has a discussion.

3. This need not be further elaborated. A useful discussion of Confucian humanism, in which perhaps there is an excessive emphasis on the humanist aspect of Confucian thought, can be found in Charles Moore, ed., *The Chinese Mind* (Honolulu: East–West Center Press, 1967), especially the opening chapter by Wing-tsit Chan, "Chinese Theory and Practice, with Special Reference to Humanism."

4. It should be noted that these positions were by no means mutually exclusive. Humanists would normally recognize the necessity of laws to obtain compliance from recalcitrant elements in society, while quasi-legalists would recognize the importance of personal virtue and the ultimate goals of social prosperity and contentment. But humanists would tend toward a distrust of bureaucratic pragmatism, accusing its practitioners of ignoring morality in their quest for national wealth and power, while their opponents would conceive of themselves as practical in their approach to social problems.

Chapter 2

1. Hsü Ch'in-wen, "Ts'ai hsien-sheng chan che wo ti hsin" [Mr. Ts'ai's Memory Occupies My Heart], *Yü-chou feng* [News of the World] 25 (June 1940): 384.

2. Ts'ai Yüan-p'ei, "Ts'ai Chieh-min hsien-sheng tzu-chuan chih i-chang" [A Chapter in the Autobiography of Ts'ai Chieh-min], *Chuan-chi wen-hsüeh* [Biographical Literature] 10, no. 1 (January 1967): 44–45; Ts'ai Shang-ssu, *Ts'ai Yüan-p'ei hsüeh-shu ssu-hsiang chuan-chi* [A Scholastic and Intellectual Biography of Ts'ai Yüan-p'ei] (Shanghai: T'ang-ti Ch'u-pan-she, 1950), p. 400. It has been mistakenly believed that Ts'ai was born in late 1867 because of confusion between the Chinese lunar calendar and the Western solar calendar. At the time of his birth, Shao-hsing was named Shan-yin district and was renamed Shao-hsing district under the Republic.

3. Ts'ai Yüan-p'ei, p. 44.

4. Evidently, Ts'ai's father had been generous with his money to his friends and in this way had squandered much of his earnings. See Ts'ai Shang-ssu, p. 92, and Huang Shih-hui, "Ts'ai Chieh-min hsien-sheng chuan-lüeh" [A Biography of Mr. Ts'ai Chieh-min], in *IWLC*, p. 541.

5. "Ts'ai Yüan-p'ei hsien-sheng nien-chi" [A Chronology of Mr. Ts'ai Yüan-p'ei], in *Ts'ai Yüan-p'ei yen-hsing-lu* [The Life and Works of Ts'ai Yüan-p'ei] (Shanghai: Kuang-yi Ch'u-pan-she, 1932), p. 7.

6. Huang Shih-hui, p. 541. Ts'ai discusses his early schooling in "Wo so shou chiu chiao-yü ti hui-i" [My Recollections of My Traditional Education], in *HC*, pp. 76–78.

7. Chih Weng, "Ts'ai Chieh-min ti chia-shih" [Household Events of Ts'ai Chieh-min], in *CC*, p. 1358.

8. Ts'ai Yüan-p'ei, "Wo tsai chiao-yü-chieh ti ching-yen" [My Experiences in Education], in *IWLC*, p. 151. Nevertheless, he did lack one important attribute of the trained Confucian literatus: his calligraphy was inadequate, a fact which occasionally shocked his acquaintances. Ch'i Weng, "Ts'ai Yüan-p'ei neng ch'ih ying-fan" [Ts'ai Yüan-p'ei Can Eat Hard Foods], in *CC*, p. 1566.

9. The Confucianist Ts'ai most admired was Liu Tsung-chou, the late Ming scholar and fellow native of Shao-hsing district. Perhaps there was an element of local pride involved, but it appears that he was attracted by Liu's courageous attempt to follow high ethical standards while a government official—often at the expense of his career. When he realized the Ming dynasty was doomed, he committed suicide.

10. Ts'ai Yüan-p'ei, "Chi Shao-hsing Chih-hsüeh Hui ti san-ta-yuan" [Recollections of the Three Great Desires of the Shao-hsing Comrade Society], in *CC*, p. 646.

11. *Yen-hsing lu*, p. 7. Many Western works not available in Chinese had been translated into Japanese. In later years, Ts'ai was known to counsel his young students to learn Japanese in order to be able to absorb Western scholarship. See Huang Yen-p'ei, "Ching-tiao wu-shih Ts'ai chieh-min hsien-sheng" [Reminiscences of My Teacher Mr. Ts'ai Chieh-min], in *CC*, p. 1496.

12. Huang Shih-hui, p. 543.

13. Ts'ai Shang-ssu, p. 49. Apparently, word reached Shao-hsing that Ts'ai had been an active member of the reform faction in Peking, because many of his acquaintances avoided him.

14. Chih Weng, "Ts'ai Chieh-min ti chin-pao yü feng-ko" [Ts'ai Chieh-min's Sensibility and Character], in *CC*, p. 1555. Perhaps Ts'ai did have a lingering hope for the Kuang-hsü emperor, since he joined a protest in 1900 against the rumored decision to depose the young monarch. See Jung-pang Lo, ed., *K'ang*

Yu-wei: A Biography and a Symposium (Tucson: Arizona University Press, 1967), p. 261.

15. Huang Shih-hui, p. 543.

16. Chih Weng, "Ts'ai Chieh-min ti chin-pao," p. 1556; Huang Shih-hui, p. 548.

17. Ts'ai Yüan-p'ei, "Wo tsai chiao-yü-chieh," p. 152. Ts'ai was already a supporter of female rights by this time. When he lost his first wife, his directive to the new intermediary was that any new wife should have unbound feet, be permitted to remarry, be able to read, and be permitted to obtain a divorce. He himself said that he would not take a concubine.

18. One source mentions that Ts'ai had to leave Nan-yang in a hurry after deliberately breaking a Buddha in a local mausoleum. The incident is reminiscent of a similar event in the youth of Sun Yat-sen. Chih-weng, "Ts'ai Chieh-min ti chin-pao," p. 1556. The South Seas Public School was founded by Sheng Hsüan-huai in 1896. For details, see Mary B. Rankin, *Early Chinese Revolutionaries: Radical Intellectuals in Shanghai and Chekiang, 1902–1911* (Cambridge: Harvard University Press, 1971), pp. 61–62.

19. Rankin, *Early Chinese Revolutionaries*, pass.

20. There has been some controversy over whether the organization was originally revolutionary in tone. See Rankin, p. 61. In any event, it became a revolutionary organ soon after its founding, and many participants have seen it in those terms from the beginning.

21. Sun Te-chung, *Ts'ai Yüan-p'ei chiao-yü hsüeh-shuo* [The Educational Thought of Ts'ai Yüan-p'ei] (Taipei: Fu-hsing Shu-chü, 1956), pp. 6–7; Huang, p. 545. The school had originated in the winter of 1901 with Chiang Kuan-yün and Wu Mu-shan, two local monks. It became a girls' school when Ts'ai, Chang, Ch'en Meng-p'o, and Lin Shao-ch'uan began to take part. The Patriotic Girls' School was supported by Lo Chio-ling. When Chiang Kuan-yün went to Japan, Ts'ai took over the direction of the school; Li Shou-k'ung states that Lo Chio-ling provided financial support for the new Patriotic Academy as well. See Li Shou-k'ung, *Chung-kuo ko-ming-shih* [A History of the Chinese Revolution] (Taipei: Chung-yang-she, 1965), p. 49. The girls' school survived the revolutionary period but in later years had no revolutionary connections.

22. Rankin, p. 73.

23. A speech which Ts'ai gave at one of these meetings is in *CC*, pp. 698–99. He demanded the convening of a people's assembly in Shanghai in order to discuss national and foreign affairs.

24. Chang Wen-po, *Wu Ching-heng hsien-sheng chuan-chi* [A Biography of Wu Ching-heng] (Taipei: Chung-kuo Kuo-min-tang Chung-yang Wei-yuan-hui, 1964), p. 9. For details of the dispute, see Huang, p. 546, and *HC*, pp. 102–3. This was apparently the beginning of the long dispute between Chang T'ai-yen and Wu Chih-hui. Ts'ai said that it had been caused by tension and a dispute over the importance of Chinese literature. Ideologically, Ts'ai found himself allied with Wu against Chang. Ts'ai Yüan-p'ei, "Tu Chang Shih so-tso *Tsou Jung chuan*" [On Reading the *Biography of Tsou Jung* by Mr. Chang], in *CC*, pp. 450–52.

25. The journal has recently been given attention in many English sources. See Harold Z. Schriffrin, *Sun Yat-sen and the Origins of the Chinese Revolution*

110

(Berkeley: University of California Press, 1968), pp. 265–66. The *Su-pao* was discussed in detail by Y. C. Wang, in "The Su-pao Case: A Study of Foreign Pressure, Intellectual Fermentation, and Dynastic Decline," *Monumenta Serica* 24 (1965): 84–129. For the most complete treatment of the events leading to the arrest, see Rankin, pp. 83–95.

26. *Chih-hui hsien-sheng i-p'ien chung-yao hui-i* [A Collection of Important Reminiscences by Mr. Chih-hui] (Taipei: World Book, 1964), pp. 95–96.

27. Ts'ai Shang-ssu, p. 198. Included in the original list to the viceroy were Ts'ai, Wu Chih-hui, Chang T'ai-yen, and Tsou Jung.

28. Chih Weng, "Ts'ai Chieh-min ti," p. 1557; Ts'ai changed his name to Ts'ai Chen, but refused to change his surname. "That," he said with dignity, "is something you cannot do at your leisure." Ts'ai's acceptance of the post of translator at the bureau did not mean his German was adequate to the task. Unemployed scholars were often given sinecure positions at the bureau to tide them over between jobs; Huang Shih-hui, p. 547.

29. Huang Shih-hui, p. 547. Ts'ai has left us with a vague indication of his feelings at this time. See his short story "Hsin-nien meng" [Dream of a New Year], in *CC*, pp. 439–47. In this story, the hero arrives at his home in China just as the Russo-Japanese War has opened on Chinese territory. He sees the home folk living their usual lives, sacrificing to the gods, drinking wine, dunning for debts, and not even bothering to read the papers. Frustrated, Ts'ai's hero leaves town, ruminating on how wonderful it would be if people would take their nation and humanity as seriously as they take their family problems.

30. Chih Weng, "Ts'ai Chieh-min ti," p. 1558. It is too bad Ts'ai left his articles unsigned. The only contribution recognized as his is "Dream of a New Year," which appeared in serial form beginning 17 February 1904.

31. Michael Gasster, *Chinese Intellectuals and the Revolution of 1911: The Birth of Modern Chinese Radicalism* (Seattle: University of Washington Press, 1969), p. 45. Rankin develops evidence that the inspiration originally came from older groups in Japan, anxious to set up a new revolutionary organization on the mainland. By this interpretation, Ts'ai, though nominally head of the organization, was not its founding father or the motive force behind it. I would tend to agree. See Rankin, pp. 104–5; Ts'ai Shang-ssu, pp. 408–9.

32. Ts'ai Yüan-p'ei, "Wo tsai chiao-yü-chieh," p. 154; Huang, p. 548. It is pathetic to read of the frustrations suffered by the group. Ts'ai was responsible for renting a room, and he introduced an explosives expert to the assassination group. After learning how to make explosives, they discovered that they had no cartridges. When some members brought a few shells from Tokyo, they turned out to be damaged. Yang Tu-sheng tried to improve the quality of the work, but soon went north in anger and joined Wu Yüeh in Paoting. Wu considered going to Shanghai, but he changed his mind and began preparations for the assassination of the group being sent to Europe to study constitutional methods.

33. Chih Weng, "Ts'ai Chieh-min ti," p. 1558.

34. There remain a number of unanswered questions surrounding this period. Chiang Wei-ch'iao says that the Restoration Society changed its name to the Revolutionary Alliance, thus implying the elimination of the Restoration Society organization. See Chiang Wei-ch'iao, "Min-kuo chiao-yü tsung-chang

Ts'ai Yüan-p'ei" [Republican Education Minister Ts'ai Yüan-p'ei], in *IWLC*, p. 561. Other sources indicate, however, that the group remained a distinct organization, with Ts'ai himself stating on one occasion that he had to mediate between the two groups. At the very least, the Restoration Society members, including Liu Shih-p'ei and Chang T'ai-yen, maintained their separate identity within the new organization.

35. Ts'ai Yüan-p'ei, "Shih ch'ou-man" [A Discussion of "Hate Manchus"], in *CC*, pp. 437–39, 439–51.

36. Huang Yen-p'ei, p. 1497.

37. Huang Yen-p'ei, p. 1496. This sentiment is also expressed in "Dream of a New Year."

Chapter 3

1. One source states that Ts'ai was victimized by an expectant *tao-t'ai* who hoped to capitalize on Ts'ai's connections in Peking as a Hanlin scholar and offered to subsidize him in Europe. When the job did not materialize, he backed out and Ts'ai was left short of funds in Germany. Consequently, Minister Sun granted him a sinecure at the Chinese legation. See Chih Weng, "Ts'ai Chieh-min ti," p. 1558.

2. Hsü Ti-shan, "Ts'ai Chieh-min hsien-sheng ti chu shu" [The Writings of Mr. Ts'ai Chieh-min], citing *Tung-fang tsa-chih* [Eastern Miscellany] 37, no. 8 (1940); see also *IWLC*, pp. 529–30.

3. For Ts'ai's translation from the Japanese, see *CC*, pp. 252–99.

4. Peter Kropotkin, *Mutual Aid* (New York: Mclure Phillips, 1902).

5. See "Spirit of Revolt," in Roger N. Baldwin, ed., *Kropotkin's Revolutionary Pamphlets* (New York: Benjamin Blom, 1968), pp. 35–43.

6. Paul A. Cohen, "Wang T'ao's Perspective on a Changing World," in Albert Feuerwerker, et al., eds., *Approaches to Modern Chinese History* (Berkeley: University of California Press, 1967), pp. 155–56.

7. Joseph R. Levenson, *Liang Ch'i-ch'ao and the Mind of Modern China* (Cambridge: Harvard University Press, 1953), p. 117, citing Liang Ch'i-ch'ao, *Tzu-yu Shu* [Book on Freedom] 45.24b. For a recent discussion of Liang's move away from morality, see Hao Chang, *Liang Ch'i-ch'ao and Intellectual Tradition in China* (Cambridge: Harvard University Press, 1971), pp. 87–90.

8. There are few detailed studies of the Chinese anarchist movement and the New Century group. For a brief analysis, see Robert A. Scalapino and George T. Yu, *The Chinese Anarchist Movement* (Berkeley: University of California Press, 1961).

9. For Yen and Liang's views, see Hao Chang, *Liang Ch'i-ch'ao*, p. 88; and Schwartz, p. 57.

10. Ts'ai Yüan-p'ei, "Hsüeh-feng tsa-chih fa-k'an-ts'e" [Foreword to *Education Trends* Magazine], in *CC*, pp. 932–33.

11. Ts'ai Yüan-p'ei, "Tendencies toward Harmony Between Eastern and Western Political Ideas," *Chinese Social and Political Science Review* 3, no. 1 (March 1918): 41–49.

12. Ts'ai Yüan-p'ei, "Shih-chieh-kuan yü jen-sheng-kuan" [World View and Life View], in *CC*, pp. 459–63.

13. Ts'ai Yüan-p'ei, "Chung-kuo ti wen-i chung-hsing" [The Chinese Literary and Artistic Revival], in *CC*, pp. 809–10.

14. Ts'ai Yüan-p'ei, "Chung-kuo ti wen-i," pp. 809–10, 812.

15. Ts'ai Yüan-p'ei, "Tui ch'u-kuo liu-Mei hsüeh-sheng chih hsi-wang" [Hopes for Students Going to America to Study], in *IWLC*, pp. 143–46; "K'o-hsueh chih hsiu-yang" [The Cultivation of Science], in *IWLC*, pp. 474–77.

16. For Liang's views on Buddhism, see Levenson, p. 132. For Chang's, see Gasster, pp. 209–10.

17. Anarchist Wu Chih-hui is a good example. See the analysis by D.W.Y. Kwok in *Scientism in Chinese Thought, 1900–1950* (New Haven: Yale University Press, 1965), pp. 42–55.

18. Peter Kropotkin, "Modern Science and Anarchism," in Baldwin, *Kropotkin*, p. 150.

19. Ts'ai Yüan-p'ei, "Tsai hsin-chiao-tzu-yu-hui chih yen-shuo" [Speech at the Religious Freedom Conference], in *CC*, pp. 724–25.

20. Friedrich Paulsen, *Introduction to Philosophy*, trans. Frank Thilly (New York: Henry Holt, 1895), pp. 58–111. This study provides an extensive discussion on epistemology; *Immanuel Kant: His Life and Writings* (New York: Creighton, 1902), pp. 310–11.

21. Paulsen, *Immanuel Kant*, p. 217.

22. Paulsen, *Immanuel Kant*, p. iii.

23. Ts'ai Yüan-p'ei, "Shih-chieh-kuan," pp. 459–63.

24. Ts'ai Yüan-p'ei, "Tui-yü chiao-yü fang-chen chih i-chien" [My Views on the Aims of Education], in *CC*, p. 455; *Che-hsüeh ta-kang* [Introduction to Philosophy] (Shanghai: Commercial Press, 1931), p. 29.

25. Ts'ai Yüan-p'ei, "Tui-yü chiao-yü," p. 455.

26. Ts'ai Yüan-p'ei, "Tsai hsin-chiao," pp. 724–25.

27. Ts'ai Yüan-p'ei, "I mei-yü tai tsung-chiao-shuo" [Replacing Religion with Aesthetics], in *CC*, p. 732.

28. Ts'ai Yüan-p'ei, article in *Shao-nien Chung-kuo* [Young China], vol. 3, no. 1 (1921).

29. Ts'ai Yüan-p'ei, "Mei-yü tai tsung-chiao-shuo" [Replacing Religion with Aesthetics], cited in Ts'ai Shang-ssu, *Ts'ai Yüan-p'ei*, pp. 370–71. This article is apparently not the same as that cited in note 27, and I have been unable to locate it elsewhere; see also Ts'ai's article in *Young China*.

30. Ts'ai Yüan-p'ei, "Shih-chieh-kuan," pp. 459–60.

31. Ts'ai Yüan-p'ei, "Tui-yü chiao-yü," pp. 455–56.

32. Ts'ai Yüan-p'ei, *Chung-kuo lün-li-hsüeh-shih* [A History of Chinese Ethics] (Taipei: Chung-yang Wen-wu Kung-ying-she, 1960), p. 25.

33. Liang Ch'i-ch'ao is the most prominent example of this tendency. See his "Lün Kung-te" [Discussion of Public Morality], in *Yin-ping-shih ch'uan-chi* [A Collection from the Ice-drinker's Studio] (Taipei: Ta-tung Shu-chü, 1964), p. 7; see also "Hsin-min-i" [The Concept of the New Man], in *Collection*, pp. 1–67.

34. Ts'ai Yüan-p'ei, "Hsin-nien meng" [Dream of a New Year], in *CC*, pp. 439–40.

35. Paulsen, *Immanuel Kant*, pp. x–xi.

36. Ts'ai Yüan-p'ei, *Che-hsüeh ta-kang*, p. 76; "Shih-chieh-kuan," pp. 461–62.

37. Ts'ai Yüan-p'ei, "Tui-yü chiao-yü," p. 454.

38. Ts'ai Yüan-p'ei, *Che-hsüeh ta-kang*, p. 69.

39. Ts'ai Yüan-p'ei, "Ts'ai Chieh-min hsien-sheng tzu-chuan chih i-chang" [A Chapter in the Autobiography of Mr. Ts'ai Chieh-min], in *Ts'ai Yüan-p'ei tzu-shu* [Ts'ai Yüan-p'ei's Autobiographical Writings] (Taipei: Chuan-chi Wen-hsüeh Ch'u-pan-she, 1967), p. 44.

40. Schwartz, pp. 103–12.

41. These essays can be found in *CC*, pp. 190–220.

42. Ts'ai Yüan-p'ei, "I-wu yü ch'uan-li" [Duties and Privileges], in *CC*, pp. 786–87; "Shih-chieh-kuan," p. 462.

43. Joseph R. Levenson, *Confucian China and its Modern Fate: The Problem of Intellectual Continuity* (London: Routledge and Kegan Paul, 1958), pp. 110–14.

44. Ts'ai Yüan-p'ei, "Wen-ming chih hsiao-hua" [The Digestion of Civilization], in *CC*, p. 643.

45. Ts'ai Yüan-p'ei, "Tu-wei po-shih liu-shih sheng-jih wan-ts'an-hui yen-shuo-ts'e" [A Speech Given at the Evening Banquet on the Occasion of the Sixtieth Birthday of Doctor Dewey], in *IWLC*, p. 329; "San-shih-wu-nien lai Chung-kuo chih hsin-wen-hua" [The New Culture of the Last Thirty-five Years in China], in *CC*, pp. 612–13.

46. Levenson, *Confucian China*, p. 111.

47. It is interesting to note, however, that one recent scholar denies the relevance of the argument to Liang himself. See Philip Huang, *Liang Ch'i-ch'ao and Chinese Liberalism* (Seattle: University of Washington Press, 1972), pp. 203–4.

48. See Ts'ai Yüan-p'ei, "Chung-kuo ti wen-i," p. 809.

49. Professor Michael Gasster has made this contention the theme of a provocative article. See "Reform and Revolution in China's Political Modernization," in Mary A. Wright, ed., *China in Revolution: The First Phase, 1900–1913* (New Haven: Yale University Press, 1969), pp. 67–96.

Chapter 4

1. A number of his letters from this period survive. In one to Wu Chih-hui, he made several suggestions regarding the possibility of purchasing weapons in Germany. In another, he disclosed his initial distrust of Yüan Shih-k'ai, who was then negotiating with Sun's government in Nanking. Ts'ai said he did not see Yüan as a Tseng Kuo-fan (a staunch defender of the Manchu dynasty—WJD), nor as a George Washington. He did not believe that Yüan would betray the revolution and attempt to become the emperor. See *HC*, vol. 3, pp. 1–3.

2. Sun first offered the educational position to Chang T'ai-yen, but the legislative assembly would not accept him. Then Huang Hsing persuaded Sun to name another ex-member of the Restoration Society, Ts'ai himself. According to one source, Chang went off in high dudgeon and formed the Kung-ho-tang in retaliation. See Chih Weng, "Ts'ai Chieh-min ti chia-shih," p. 1560.

3. For Chang Chih-tung's reforms, see Tu Tso-chou, "Chin pai-nien lai Chung-kuo hsin chiao-yü chih fa-chan" [The Development of China's New Education in the Last Hundred Years], in Tu et al., eds., *Chin Pai-nien lai chih Chung-kuo chiao-yü* [Chinese Education in the Last Hundred Years] (Hong

Kong: Lung-men, 1969); William Ayers, *Chang Chih-tung and Educational Reform* (Cambridge: Harvard University Press, 1971), pp. 206–31.

4. Tu, pp. 13–14; see also Ayers, p. 245.

5. Ts'ai Yüan-p'ei, "Shih-chieh-kuan," p. 462.

6. Ts'ai Yüan-p'ei, "Tui-yü chiao-yü," *CC*, pp. 452–59.

7. Tu, p. 11.

8. Ts'ai Yüan-p'ei to Wang Ching-wei, March 1917, *CC*, p. 1062.

9. For advances in female education, see Tu, pp. 12–13; Yü Ch'ing-t'ang, "San-shih-wu nien lai Chung-kuo chih nü-tzu chiao-yü" [Female Education over the Last Thirty-five Years], in Ts'ai Yüan-p'ei et al., eds., *Wan Ch'ing san-shih-wu nien lai chih Chung-kuo chiao-yü* [Chinese Education in the Last Thirty-five Years Since the Late Ch'ing Period] (Hong Kong: Lung-men, 1969), pp. 175–214; Cyrus Peake, *Nationalism and Education in Modern China* (New York: Columbia University Press, 1932), p. 75.

10. Ts'ai Yüan-p'ei, "Pu-t'ung chiao-yü chan-hsing pan-fa" [Temporary Regulations for Ordinary Education], in *CC*, pp. 1043–44; "Tui chiao-yü tsung-chih-an chih shuo-ming" [The Explanation of the Educational Program], in *CC*, pp. 703–4. For a discussion of language reform, see John De Francis, *Nationalism and Language Reform in China* (Princeton: Princeton University Press, 1950), pp. 50–56. Ts'ai had already stated publicly that China should adopt Esperanto as a means of international communication. See "Tsai Shih-chieh-yü-hsüeh-hui chih yen-shuo" [Speech at the World Language Conference], in *CC*, pp. 699–702.

11. Ts'ai Yüan-p'ei, *Wan Ch'ing san-shih-wu*, p. 15.

12. See the diary of the conference in Shu Hsin-ch'eng, *Chung-kuo chin-tai chiao-yü-shih tzu-liao* [Research Materials on the History of Education in Modern China], 3 vols. (Peking, 1961), 1: 296–310.

13. For a discussion of Ts'ai's reformist proposals, see Robert Sakai, "*Politics and Education in Modern China*" (Ph.D. diss., Harvard University, 1953), pp. 53–54.

14. Tu, p. 13; Chiu-Sam Tsang, *Nationalism in School Education in China* (Hong Kong: South China Morning Post, 1933), p. 97.

15. Shu, vol. 1, pp. 1069–70; vol. 2, pp. 258–69.

16. In "Yüan Shih-k'ai's Rise to the Presidency," Ernest P. Young mentions other reasons for Yüan's reluctance. See Mary Wright, ed., *China in Revolution: The First Phase, 1900–1913* (New Haven: Yale University Press, 1969), p. 437.

17. Ts'ai was sent to Peking because he was a member of the old revolutionary alliance and a cabinet member. He was also chosen because of his conciliatory nature.

18. Chih Weng, "Ts'ai chieh-min ti," p. 1058. For Ts'ai's detailed description of the events, see *CC*, pp. 1461–63; see also Ts'ai Yüan-p'ei, "Kao ch'uan-kuo wen" [A Declaration to All the Chinese People], in *Ts'ai Yüan-p'ei hsüan chi* (Peking: Chung-hua Shu-chü, 1959). This should not be confused with *HC*, which was published on the island of Taiwan.

19. Ts'ai Shang-ssu, *Ts'ai Yüan-p'ei hsüeh-shu ssu-hsiang chuan-chi* (A Scholastic and Intellectual Biography of Ts'ai Yüan-p'ei] (Shanghai: T'ang-ti Ch'u-pan-she, 1950), p. 60.

20. *CC*, p. 689.

21. Ts'ai Shang-ssu, *Ts'ai Yüan-p'ei hsüeh-shu*, p. 145.

22. *CC*, p. 687.

23. George T. Yu, *Party Politics in Republican China* (Berkeley: University of California Press, 1966), p. 92, citing *Chung-kuo T'ung-meng-hui Yueh-chia pu tsa-chih*, no. 7 (September 1912), pp. 4–5. See also Ts'ai Yüan-p'ei, "Sung Chiao-jen chu 'Wo chih li-shih' hsü" [Preface to Sun Chiao-jen's "My History"], in *CC*, p. 949.

24. See Ts'ai Yüan-p'ei to Yüan Shih-k'ai, *Ko-ming wen-hsien* [Materials on the Revolution] Committee on Editing Party History Materials, vol. 44.

25. *Yen-hsing lu*, p. 14.

Chapter 5

1. Ts'ai Yüan-p'ei, "Wo tsai Pei-ching Ta-hsüeh ti ching-yen" [My Experience at Peking University], in *CC*, pp. 629–30.

2. Lo Chia-lün, "Ts'ai Yüan-p'ei hsien-sheng yü Pei-ching Ta-hsüeh," [Ts'ai Yüan-p'ei and Peking University], in *CC*, p. 1451.

3. Ts'ai Yüan-p'ei, "Chiu-jen Pei-ching Ta-hsüeh hsiao-chang chih yen-shuo-ts'e" [A Speech on Assuming the Chancellorship of Peking University], in *CC*, pp. 721–23.

4. Ts'ai Yüan-p'ei to Wang Ching-wei, January 1917, *CC*, p. 1062. Ts'ai tried to persuade Wang that politicians were not as bad as they used to be.

5. Ts'ai Yüan-p'ei to Wu Chih-hui, 18 January 1917, *CC*, p. 1063. Ts'ai informed Wu that there were two reasons for the university's sad state of affairs: the confusion and inadequacy of the courses, and the corruption and lack of discipline. The answer, therefore, was to encourage pure scholarship and attract model students.

6. Much of Ts'ai's program for the reorganization of the administration was based on the German system of self-government. See *CC*, pp. 1066–67. For his attitude toward speaking clubs, see his December 1917 statement in *CC*, p. 1077.

7. See "Wo tsai Pei-ching," p. 630.

8. A list of new faculty members brought to Peita can be found in "Wo tsai Pei-ching," p. 635.

9. For Li's ideas at this period, see Maurice Meisner, *Li Ta-chao and the Origins of Chinese Marxism* (Cambridge: Harvard University Press, 1967), p. 47.

10. Jerome Grieder, *Hu Shih and the Chinese Renaissance* (Cambridge: Harvard University Press, 1970), pp. 324–25.

11. Hu Shih, "Fei ko-jen chu-i ti hsin sheng-huo" [The New Life of Non-individualism], in *Hsin sheng-huo lün-ts'ung* [Essays on the New Life] (Shanghai: Ch'ing-men Ch'u-pan-she, 1936), pp. 5–19.

12. Mu Hsin [pseud.], "Chiao-yü yü de-mo-k'o-la-hsi" [Education and Democracy], citing *Chiao-yü tsa-chih* [Educational Review] 11, no. 9 (20 September 1919); Grieder, p. 326.

13. The best examples—Ch'en Tu-hsiu, Lo Wen-kan, and the Noulens—will be discussed later. Ts'ai did take pains to draw a fine distinction between freedom and license, and frequently quoted Confucius to buttress his points. See "Chi so pu yü wu shih yü jen" [Do not do unto others that which you would

not have them do unto you], in *CC*, pp. 194–95; see also "Tzu-yu yü fang-ts'ung" [Freedom and License], in *CC*, pp. 208–9.

14. Ts'ai Yüan-p'ei, "I-wu yü ch'uan-li" [Responsibility and Privilege], in *CC*, pp. 786–88.

15. When he supported the formation of the Society for the Propagation of Virtue [*Chin-te-hui*] at Peita, he clearly expressed his desire to achieve such a moral transformation. See his speech, "Pei-ching Ta-hsueh chih Chin-te-hui chih-ch'ü shu" [The Essential Meaning of the Peking University Society for the Promotion of Virtue], in *CC*, pp. 469–72.

16. See Kwok, *Scientism in Chinese Thought*; see also Ts'ai Yüan-p'ei, "Tsai Hsin-chiao Tzu-yu-hui chih yen-shuo" [Speech at the Religious Freedom Conference], in *CC*, pp. 724–25.

17. Ts'ai Yüan-p'ei, "Hsin wen-hua yün-tung pu-yao wang-liao mei-yü" [The New Culture Movement Should Not Forget Aesthetics], in *CC*, pp. 495–96. Ts'ai feared that the following problems would occur: sacrifice of principle through allowing yourself petty advantages; petty motives behind good principles which would eventually be discovered by the reactionaries; and impatience to achieve utopia which would lead to discouragement when you face obstacles. See his "Mei-yü yü jen-sheng [Aesthetics and Life], in *CC*, p. 639.

18. Ts'ai Yüan-p'ei, "Mei-yü chiao-yü shih-shih ti fang-fa" [A Method for Realizing Aesthetics Education], in *CC*, pp. 535–40.

19. Ts'ai Yüan-p'ei, "Wo chih Ou-chan kuan" [My View of the European War], in *CC*, pp. 710–13. For a detailed exposition of his views on aesthetics, see W. Duiker, "The Aesthetics Philosophy of Ts'ai Yüan-p'ei," *Philosophy East and West* 22, no. 4 (October 1972): 385–401.

20. Ts'ai Yüan-p'ei, "Ho wei wen-hua" [What is Culture], in *Ts'ai Yüan-p'ei hsüan-chi* [The Selected Works of Ts'ai Yüan-p'ei], pp. 157–58; see also Chiu-sam Tsang, *Nationalism in School Education in China* (Hong Kong: South China Morning Post, 1933), pp. 97–109.

21. His most prominent articles were "Ou-chan hou chih chiao-yü wen-t'i" [Problems of Education after the War] and "Hsin chiao-yü yü chiu chiao-yü chih ch'i-tien" [The Differences Between the New and the Old Education], in *CC*, pp. 775–79 and 737–40.

22. See Tu Tso-chou, "Chin-pai-nien lai chih Chung-kuo," p. 15.

23. For Ts'ai's support of Wu's proposal, see his "Kuo-yü chiang-hsi-so chih yen-shuo" [Speech at the National Language Study Society], in *CC*, pp. 793–96. See also De Francis, pp. 54–56.

24. De Francis, pp. 51–52. See also Ts'ai Yüan-p'ei, "Han-tzu kai-ko-shuo" [Speech on the Reform of the Han Characters], in *HC*, p. 204.

25. For this issue, see *Wan Ch'ing san-shih-wu-nien lai chih Chung-kuo chiao-yü* [Chinese Education in the Thirty-five Years Since the Late Ch'ing] (Hong Kong: Lung-men, 1969), pp. 335–72; De Francis, p. 68.

26. Ts'ai Yüan-p'ei, "Kuo-wen chih chiang-lai" [The Future of the National Language], in *CC*, p. 783.

27. Peake, p. 147.

28. The society was originally established in 1909, but was temporarily disbanded. See *New Youth* 3, no. 2 (1 April 1917); see also Chow Tse-tsung, *The May Fourth Movement* (Cambridge: Harvard University Press, 1960), p. 36.

29. The association was originally founded as a beancurd factory by Li Shih-tseng. See Shu Hsin-ch'eng, *Chung-kuo chin-tai chiao-yü-shih tzu-liao* [Materials on the History of Education in Modern China], 3 vols. (Peking, 1961), 1: 877–82.

30. In a speech, "Kuo-wai Lao-kung Chien-hsüeh hui yü Kuo-nei Kung-hsüeh Hu-chu-t'uan" [The Labor Frugal Study Society Abroad and the Mutual Assistance Labor Teams at Home], Ts'ai praised the program and suggested its use in China. See *IWLC*, pp. 174–79.

31. Chow Tse-tsung, pp. 191, 198.

32. Ts'ai Yüan-p'ei, "Wo tsai Pei-ching," pp. 629–30; Tu, p. 13.

33. Women started as auditors in 1919. See "Wo tsai Pei-ching." See also Ts'ai Yüan-p'ei, "Yang-ch'eng yu-mei ssu-hsiang" [Improving Superior and Brilliant Thought], in *Ts'ai Yüan-p'ei yen-hsing-lu* [The Life and Works of Ts'ai Yüan-p'ei] (Shanghai: Kuang-yi Ch'u-pan-she, 1932), p. 4.

34. Ts'ai Yüan-p'ei, "Yang-ch'eng yu-mei," p. 4.

35. See Ts'ai Yüan-p'ei, *Wan Ch'ing san shih-wu*, p. 206.

36. Chow Tse-tsung, pp. 66–67.

37. Ts'ai's reply can be found in *IWLC*, pp. 32–36.

38. The Association for a Confucian Religion was led by traditionalists who were attempting to transform Confucianism into the official religion of China.

39. See Chow Tse-tsung, p. 72.

40. As Chow pointed out, Ts'ai had to avoid a blanket endorsement of the movement, given the nature of the circumstances. This was probably a factor hindering a more honest response.

Chapter 6

1. Li Ta-chao, "Shu-min ti sheng-li" [The Victory of the Masses], *New Youth* 5, no. 5 (15 October 1918).

2. Ts'ai Yüan-p'ei, "Hei-an yü kuang-ming ti hsiao-chang" [The Interaction of the Forces of Light and Darkness], in *CC*, pp. 765–67.

3. Ch'en Tu-hsiu, "Chin-jih Chung-kuo chih cheng-chih wen-t'i" [The Political Problems of China Today], *New Youth* 5, no. 1 (15 July 1918).

4. Ts'ai Yüan-p'ei, "*Kuo-min tsa-chih* hsü" [Preface to *National* Magazine], in *CC*, p. 946.

5. Ts'ai Yüan-p'ei, "Wo tsai Pei-ching," p. 633.

6. Chih Weng, "Ts'ai Chieh-min ti . . . ," p. 1563. See also pp. 1007 and 1599.

7. For Ts'ai's visit to the chief of police, see *CC*, p. 1563. In a speech in Hunan Province in February 1921, Ts'ai elaborated on his views regarding student riots: "After May 4, society greatly respected students, but many ill effects have appeared more recently. The students have begun to think of themselves as omnipotent, and often think they have the right to interfere with society on all sorts of political matters. . . . Students cannot by themselves resolve the problems of a nation, since a student movement is always on the outside, so they cannot directly solve all problems. Therefore, frequent movements are unnecessary. . . ." See "Tui-yü shih-fan-sheng ti hsi-wang" [Hopes for a Model Student Life], in *Ts'ai Yüan-p'ei hsüan-chi* [A Selection of the Writings of Ts'ai Yüan-p'ei] (Peking: Chung-hua Shu-chü, 1959), p. 158.

8. Sun Te-chung, "Wu-ssu ai-kuo yün-tung chi-yao" [Record of the May Fourth Patriotic Movement], in *CC,* pp. 1103 and 1108.

9. In a telegram to the government, however, Ts'ai implied that he might be persuaded to return. The telegram is in *CC,* p. 1110.

10. John Dewey, *Letters from China and Japan* (New York: Dutton, 1920), pp. 288–89.

11. There are several explanations for Ts'ai's resignation. Ts'ai Shang-ssu claims that he was afraid that his dismissal would provoke the students to greater riots. See Ts'ai Shang-ssu, *Ts'ai Yüan-p'ei hsüeh-shu,* p. 66. His assistant Chiang Monlin claims that Ts'ai was "shocked" by the violence of the movement, thus stimulating his resignation. Chiang Monlin, *Tides from the West* (New Haven: Yale University Press, 1947), p. 208.

12. Ts'ai Yüan-p'ei, "Kao Pei-ching Ta-hsüeh hsüeh-sheng yü ch'uan-kuo hsüeh-sheng lien-ho-hui hsü" [A Letter to the United Conference of Peking University Students and Other Students from around the Nation], in *CC,* p. 1111.

13. Ts'ai Yüan-p'ei, "Wo tsai Pei-ching," p. 634.

14. Ts'ai Yüan-p'ei, "Hung-shui yü meng-shou" [Floods and Wild Beasts], *New Youth* 7, no. 5 (1 April 1920).

15. See the article by Lin Yu-sheng, "Radical Iconoclasm in the May Fourth Period and the Future of Chinese Liberalism," in Benjamin Schwartz, ed., *Reflections on the May Fourth Movement: A Symposium* (Cambridge: Harvard East Asian Monographs, 1972), pp. 24–25.

16. Chow Tse-tsung, p. 174, citing *New Youth* (1 December 1919), pp. 1–4.

17. Ts'ai suggested the petition, but Hu Shih drafted it. Ts'ai Shang-ssu, *Ts'ai Yüan-p'ei hsüeh-shu,* pp. 156–57. English excerpts are in Grieder, pp. 191–93.

18. Ts'ai Yüan-p'ei, "Min-kuo shih-erh-nien i-yüeh, erh-shih-san-jih wei Lo Wen-kan tsao fei-fa tai-pu-an k'ang-i hsüan-yen" [A Declaration of Protest against the Illegal Arrest on 23 January 1922 of Lo Wen-kan], in *CC,* pp. 541–43.

19. Ts'ai had recently married a woman surnamed Chou, an old acquaintance who had studied at the Patriotic Girls' School. His first wife had died while he was in Europe. See Ts'ai Yüan-p'ei, "Wo tsai chiao-yü-chieh," p. 682.

20. Hu Shih, "Ts'ai Yüan-p'ei shih hsiao-chi ma?" [Does Ts'ai Yüan-p'ei Have a Negative Attitude?], *Nu-li chou-pao* [Struggle Weekly], no. 40 (4 February 1923).

21. Leon Wieger, *Chine Moderne* [Hien-hien], 8 vols., vol. 3, p. 395; see also Chiang Monlin, *Kuo-tu shih-tai chih ssu-hsiang yü chiao-yü* [The Thought and • Education of a Transitional Age] (Taipei: Shih-chieh Shu-chü, 1962), p. 97.

22. See *HC,* vol. 1, pp. 20–24.

23. For details of the program, see Robert Sakai, *"Politics and Education in Modern China"* (Ph.D. diss., Harvard University, 1953), p. 144.

24. Peake, pp. 147–53. See also the discussion by Tatsuro and Sumiko Yamamoto, "The Anti-Christian Movement in China, 1922–1927," *Far Eastern Quarterly* 12, no. 2 (February 1953): 133–48.

25. C. S. Chang, "The Anti-Religious Movement," *The Chinese Recorder* 14, no. 8 (August 1923), p. 460.

26. Neander S. H. Chang, "The Anti-Religious Movement," *The Chinese Social and Political Science Review* 7, no. 2 (February 1923): 103–12.

27. Ts'ai Yüan-p'ei, "Chiao-yü tu-li-i" [The Independence of Education], in *CC*, pp. 523–24.

28. W. H. Kiang, *The Chinese Student Movement* (Morningside Heights: King's Crown Press, 1948), pp. 89–90.

29. Paul K. T. Sih, ed., *The Strenuous Decade: China's Nation-Building Efforts, 1927–1937* (New York: St. John's University Press, 1970), p. 296; Tsi C. Wang, *The Youth Movement in China* (New York: New Republic, 1928), p. 212.

30. There are indications, too, that his decision stemmed from a personal fatigue with the rough-and-tumble world of politics, and a desire for a rest. See Ts'ai Yüan-p'ei, "Min-kuo shih-erh-nien," pp. 541–43.

31. Hu Shih, "Ts'ai Yüan-p'ei ti 'pu-ho-tso-chu-i' " [Ts'ai Yüan-p'ei's Doctrine of Passive Resistance], in *CC*, p. 1432.

Chapter 7

1. Leon Wieger, *Chine Moderne*, vol. 5, p. 195, citing *Min-kuo jih-pao* [Republic Daily], 18 May 1924.

2. T'ang Leang-li, *The Inner History of the Chinese Revolution* (London: Routledge and Sons, 1930), pp. 320–26.

3. Huang Chi-lung, "Ts'ai Yüan-p'ei yü kuo-fu ti kuan-hsi" [The Relations between Ts'ai Yüan-p'ei and the Father of the Republic], in *CC*, pp. 1407–9. Ts'ai was not always in agreement with Sun during this period. In June 1922, he attempted to persuade Sun to come to Peking after the defeat of Tuan Ch'i-jui and the accession of Li Yüan-hung to the presidency. But Sun continued to defend Ts'ai within the party and, according to Huang, pressed for his appointment to the Central Supervisory Committee over objections in the party. Two criticisms were brought against Ts'ai, that he had served under the Peking government as chancellor, and that he had encouraged student radicalism, causing irreparable damage to Confucianism. Despite these objections, Sun appointed him and defended his revolutionary accomplishments in education.

4. T'ang Leang-li, pp. 320–26.

5. In 1926, Ts'ai had been created a full member of the supervisory committee at the second session of the Central Executive Committee. See Yang Yü-chiung, *Chung-kuo cheng-tang-shih* [A History of Chinese Political Parties] (Shanghai: Commercial Press, 1937).

6. Arthur N. Holcombe, *The Chinese Revolution* (Cambridge: Harvard University Press, 1930), p. 230. See also T'ang, p. 324. T'ang states that the Elder Statesmen preferred regional autonomy in accordance with their "anarchist tendencies" and personal rather than party rule, as advocated by the radical wing. He also claims elsewhere that they had developed a personal antipathy to Wang Ching-wei. Although they had been on close terms in earlier years, it appears that Wang and Ts'ai drifted apart during this period. Ts'ai always distrusted centralized political control and may have clashed with Wang over the issue. Wang's own views had drifted away from anarchism since the early republican period.

7. See W. H. Kiang, p. 79.

8. Ts'ai's article is in *La Revue Bleue,* Paris, located in *China Yearbook* (Shanghai: Commercial Press, 1925), p. 569. See also his "Chung-kuo ti wen-i chunghsing" [China's Literary and Artistic Renaissance], in *CC,* pp. 813–14.

9. Wieger, vol. 6, p. 73.

10. Ts'ai Yüan-p'ei, "Chung-yang tang-wu-hsüeh-hsiao t'o-pieh ch'u-fen-pu ch'eng-li ti i-i" [The Meaning Behind the Foundation of the Special Branch of the Central Party School], in *CC,* p. 818. Ts'ai paid a price for his new-found conservatism. Previously, his colleagues had considered him to be a member of the progressive wing of the nationalist movement. By the spring of 1927, however, leftist students were calling him an opportunist. This must have hurt, for on one occasion, Ts'ai lost his composure during a speech and shouted back to a heckler: "When I began participating in revolutionary activities, you weren't even born!" See Ts'ao Chien, "Ts'ai Chieh-min hsien-sheng ti feng-ku" [The Character of Mr. Ts'ai Chieh-min], in *CC,* p. 1598.

11. Holcombe, p. 230.

12. T'ang Leang-li, pp. 265–66.

13. Yang Yü-ch'iung, *Chung-kuo cheng-tang shih* [A History of Political Parties in China] (Shanghai: Commercial Press, 1937), p. 174.

14. Ts'ai Yüan-p'ei, "Chung-yang tang-wu," p. 818; Yang, p. 175.

15. George Sokolsky, "The KMT," in *China Yearbook* (1928), p. 1361.

16. Ts'ai Shang-ssu, *Ts'ai Yüan-p'ei hsüeh-shu,* p. 75; Tai Chin-hsieo, "The Life and Works of Ts'ai Yüan-p'ei" (Ph.D. diss., Harvard University, 1952), citing Pan Su (Li Chien-nung), *Important Events in the Last Sixty Years Since the Birth of Sun Yat-sen* (1929), p. 602.

17. Ts'ai was made a member of the committee.

18. Sokolsky, p. 1173.

19. Sokolsky, p. 1185.

20. Ts'ai Shang-ssu, *Ts'ai Yüan-p'ei,* p. 30, citing Lo Ya-tzu, "Chi-nien Ts'ai Yüan-p'ei hsien-sheng" [In Memory of Mr. Ts'ai Yüan-p'ei].

21. Ts'ai, "Chung-yang," p. 818.

22. See *La Revue Bleue,* p. 569.

23. Tuan Hsi-p'eng, "Hui-i" [Reminiscences], in *IWLC,* p. 594.

24. For his government posts, see *Ts'ai Yüan-p'ei yen-hsing-lu* [The Life and Works of Ts'ai Yüan-p'ei] (Shanghai: Kuang-yi Ch'u-pan-she, 1932), introductory biographical sketch. Ts'ai discussed these complex events in "Yüeh-Ning-Han chih fen-lieh yü Chung-yang T'o-pieh Wei-yuan-hui ch'eng-li ching-kuo ch'ing-hsing" [The Events Surrounding the Split of Kwangtung, Nanking, and Hankow, and the Formation of the Central Special Committee], in *HC,* vol. 4, pp. 143–44.

25. Ts'ai Yüan-p'ei, "Chiao-yü tu-li-i," pp. 523–24.

26. Ts'ai Yüan-p'ei, "Ou-chan hou chih chiao-yü wen-t'i" [Problems of Education After the European War], in *CC,* pp. 777–78.

27. Ts'ai Yüan-p'ei et al., *Wan Ch'ing san-shih-wu-nien,* p. 107.

28. For a recent discussion of this period, see Allan B. Linden's "Politics and Education in Nationalist China," *Journal of Asian Studies* 27, no. 4 (August 1968), pp. 763–76. See also Ts'ai Yüan-p'ei, "Wo tsai chiao-yü chiehti chingyen" [My Experience in Education], in *CC,* pp. 681–83. In this article, Ts'ai

discussed the advantages of his educational system and the circumstances surrounding its adoption.

29. Chiu-Sam Tsang, *Nationalism in School Education in China* (Hong Kong: South China Morning Post, 1933), pp. 109–16.

30. Wieger, vol. 6, pp. 82–84; Peake, p. 125; see the article by Shun-sheng [pseud.], *Chüeh-wu tsa-chih* [Awakening Magazine], Wieger, vol. 6, pp. 139–40.

31. Peake, p. 127.

32. Ts'ai, "Wo tsai chiao-yü-chieh," pp. 681–83.

33. Ts'ai Yüan-p'ei, "Ta-hsüeh-yüan kung-pao fa-k'an-ts'e" [Preface to the Declaration of the University Council], in *IWLC*, pp. 354–55.

34. For a more extensive treatment of this issue, see John Israel, *Student Nationalism in China, 1927–1937* (Stanford: Stanford University Press, 1966).

35. See Ts'ai Yüan-p'ei, "Ch'ing t'ung-ling hsüeh-sheng pu-te kan-she hsiao-cheng chih t'i-an" [A Request that Students No Longer Interrupt School Administration], in *CC*, p. 832; *Wan Ch'ing san-shih-wu*, p. 113.

36. Chiu-Sam Tsang, p. 116.

37. Ts'ai Yüan-p'ei, "Yü Yeh Ch'u-tsang teng lien-shu wei t'i-ch'u shih-shih i-wu chiao-yü piao-pen chien chih pan-fa-an yüan-wen" [A Joint Proposal with Yeh Ch'u-tsang and Others on the Question of Realizing Obligatory Education], in *HC*, vol. 3, p. 163. The Second All-China Educational Conference had called for its realization within twenty years.

38. *HC*, vol. 3, p. 165; *China Yearbook* (1936), p. 37.

39. Tu Tso-chou, "Chin pai-nien lai Chung-kuo," pp. 31–32.

40. See Ts'ai Yüan-p'ei, "Yü Yeh," pp. 163–65. See also his "Tui ch'üeh-ting chiao-yü she-shih chih ch'ü-hsiang-an shuo-ming" [An Explanation of the Proposal to Define a Plan for Educational Tendencies], in *HC*, vol. 3, pp. 148–49. At this time, only 7 percent of Chinese students were in vocational schools.

41. See Ts'ai Yüan-p'ei, "Chang I 'K'o-hsüeh-chieh ti wei-jen' hsü" [Preface to Chang's Translation of 'Great Men of Science'], in *HC*, vol. 3, pp. 175–76.

42. Israel has a brief discussion of this incident. For Ts'ai's replies to reporters after the fracas, see his "Shou Pei-p'ing hsüeh-sheng-tuan wei-k'ün hou ta chi-che wen" [Answer to Reporters' Questions after Being Molested by Peiping Student Groups], in *CC*, pp. 869–70.

43. Ts'ai Yüan-p'ei, "Hsi-sheng hsüeh-yeh sun-shih yü shih t'u hsiang-teng" [The Loss of Territory and the Sacrifice of Educational Careers are the Same], in *CC*, pp. 866–69.

44. *HC*, vol. 4, pp. 78–79.

45. *Yen-hsing-lu*, pp. 24–25.

46. Ts'ai Yüan-p'ei, "Chiao-chih hou chih hsiao-tu kung-tso" [The Job of Eradicating the Poison after Suppressing the Reds], in *CC*, pp. 862–63.

47. Ts'ai Yüan-p'ei, "She-hui-chu-i-shih-hsü" [Preface to *A History of Socialism*], *New Youth* 8, no. 1 (September 1920).

48. Ts'ai Shang-ssu, *Ts'ai Yüan-p'ei*, pp. 81 and 126.

49. *People's Tribune*, 30 June 1932, pp. 329–30, and 16 February 1937, pp. 69–72.

50. Ts'ai Shang-ssu, *Ts'ai Yüan-p'ei*, pp. 80 and 83.

51. Lin said that he and Ts'ai were "exploited without our knowledge," and that he woke up to the leftist nature of the organization when he saw Soong Ch'ing-ling and the "Red Lady" Agnes Smedley rushing to Nanking when the Noulens case broke. See Lin Yu-t'ang, "Chi Ts'ai Chieh-min hsien-sheng" [A Recollection of Mr. Ts'ai Chieh-min], in *CC*, pp. 1471–72; Hu Shih also broke with the organization. Many other intellectuals were cautious and stayed away entirely; one source says that Ts'ai's friends were "mortified" by his participation in the league.

52. Ts'ai Shang-ssu, *Ts'ai Yüan-p'ei*, p. 162.

53. There are indications that Ts'ai had trouble with radical elements in the alliance. During one of the meetings, strikes and rioting were suggested. Ts'ai retorted angrily: "We are talking about rights, and should make our demands legally, by use of the Three People's Principles!" See Ts'ao Chien, *CC*, p. 1600. See also Ts'ai Shang-ssu, *Ts'ai Yüan-p'ei*, p. 166.

54. This speech, published in the *Chinese Social and Political Science Review*, was given in an English translation. In some places, the translation is unclear, but I have not been able to find a Chinese language original.

55. For an extended discussion of Russell's views on China, see *The Problem of China* (New York: Century, 1922), Chapter 11.

56. Ts'ai Yüan-p'ei, "Tendencies Toward Harmony between Eastern and Western Political Ideas," trans. L. K. Tao, *Chinese Social and Political Science Review* 3, no. 1 (March 1918): 41–49.

57. Ts'ai, "Chung-kuo ti wen-i," p. 809; "Chung-hua min-tsu yü chung-yung chih tao" [The Chinese Nationality and the Way of the Chung-yung], in *CC*, pp. 850–51.

58. Ts'ai Yüan-p'ei, "San-min-chu-i ti chung-ho-hsing" [The Moderate Character of the Three People's Principles], in *CC*, p. 649.

59. In "The Politics of Chiang Kai-shek," *Journal of Asian Studies* 25, no. 3 (May 1966): 431–52, Pichon Loh makes the point that Chiang maintained a centrist position in the Kuomintang regarding its political factionalism. In cultural matters, however, I think he tended to support the more traditionalist elements. For evidence regarding his views on culture, see Chiang's *China's Destiny* (New York: Roy, 1947).

60. "Chung-kuo pen-wei wen-hua chien-she hsüan-yen" [A Declaration Regarding the Construction of a Standard Culture in China], *Wen-hua chien-she* [Cultural Construction], 4, no. 1, cited in Kuo Chan-p'o, *Chin Wu-shih-nien*, p. 339.

61. *Wen-hua Chien-she*, p. 344, citing Hu Shih, "Shih-p'ing so-wei Chung-kuo pen-wei wen-hua chien-she" [A Criticism of the Declaration of the Construction of a Standard Culture in China].

62. Arguments on both sides of the issue are located in the 1 April and 8 April 1935 issues of *Kuo-wen chou-pao* [National Literature Weekly].

63. Ts'ai Yüan-p'ei, "Fu Ho Ping-sung Po-ch'eng chiao-shou tsemma-yang tso i wen-hua chien-she ti fang-an han" [A Letter Responding to the Plan of Mr. Ho Ping-sung on Cultural Construction], in *CC*, p. 1272.

64. This is further evidence of the point made earlier that he was not assuming that China had *value* to offer the West.

65. Lo Chia-lun, "Wei-ta yü tsung-kao" [Greatness and Respect], in *IWLC*, pp. 596–98 and Wang Shih-chieh, "Chui-i Ts'ai hsien-sheng" [Recollections of Mr. Ts'ai], in *IWLC*, p. 577.

66. Chou Hsin, "Ts'ai Chieh-min hsien-sheng ti tsui-hou i-yen" [The Last Words of Mr. Ts'ai Chieh-min], in *CC*, p. 1753. See also *CC*, p. 1568. Chou indicates in his reminiscence that a pathetic scene took place at Ts'ai's death-bed. Ts'ai had made a long monologue prior to his death, but because he was not wearing his false teeth, Chou was unable to understand what Ts'ai had said. The only phrase that was intelligible, and that was repeated over and over again, was "K'o-hsueh chiu kuo, mei-yu chiu kuo" [Science and aesthetics can save the nation]. Although he has tried to pass on the reformer's last wish, Chou believes that few have taken it seriously.

Chapter 8

1. Interview with *Time* reporter, cited in *CC*, pp. 907–8.